7/19

THICK

Also by Tressie McMillan Cottom

Lower Ed: The Troubling Rise of For-Profit
Colleges in the New Economy

For-Profit Universities: The Shifting Landscape
of Marketized Higher Education
(co-editor with William A. Darity Jr.)

THICK

And Other Essays

TRESSIE McMILLAN COTTOM

THE
NEW
PRESS

NEW YORK
LONDON

Requests for permission to reproduce selections from this book should be mailed to:
Permissions Department, The New Press, 120 Wall Street, 31st floor, New York, NY 10005.

Grateful acknowledgment is made to:
The Atlantic for permission to reprint "The Problem with Obama's Faith in White People,"
© 2016 by Tressie McMillan Cottom; the *New York Times* for permission to reprint
"How We Make Black Girls Grow Up Too Fast," © 2017 by Tressie McMillan Cottom;
Warner Chappell Music, Inc. for permission to use lyrics from the song "Thick & Pretty"
performed by Migos; Sony Music for permission to use lyrics from the song "Mix'd Girl"
performed by T-Pain; the Joy Harris Literary Agency, Inc. for permission to use lines from
"Those Who Love Us Never Leave Us Alone with Our Grief" by Alice Walker, the foreword
to *Barracoon: The Story of the Last "Black Cargo"* by Zora Neale Hurston (New York:
Amistad, 2018), © 2018 by Alice Walker; Curtis Brown, Ltd. for permission to use lines
from the poem "homage to my hips," copyright © 1980 by Lucille Clifton. Now appears in
The Collected Poems of Lucille Clifton 1965–2010 by Lucille Clifton, published by BOA
Editions. Reprinted by permission of Curtis Brown, Ltd.

Published in the United States by The New Press, New York, 2019

Distributed by Two Rivers Distribution

ISBN 978-1-62097-436-0 (hc)
ISBN 978-1-62097-437-7 (ebook)
CIP data is available

The New Press publishes books that promote and enrich public discussion and understanding of
the issues vital to our democracy and to a more equitable world. These books are made possible
by the enthusiasm of our readers; the support of a committed group of donors, large and small;
the collaboration of our many partners in the independent media and the not-for-profit sector;
booksellers, who often hand-sell New Press books; librarians; and above all by our authors.

www.thenewpress.com

Book design and composition by Bookbright Media
This book was set in Goudy Oldstyle and Futura

Printed in the United States of America

4 6 8 10 9 7 5 3

For Gabrielle, always.

Life, inexhaustible, goes on. And we do too. Carrying our wounds and our medicines as we go. Ours is an amazing, a spectacular, journey in the Americas. It is so remarkable one can only be thankful for it, bizarre as that may sound.

Perhaps our planet is for learning to appreciate the extraordinary wonder of life that surrounds even our suffering, and to say Yes, if through the thickest of tears.

—Alice Walker, from the
foreword to Zora Neale
Hurston's *Barracoon*

CONTENTS

Thick   1

In the Name of Beauty   33

Dying to Be Competent   73

Know Your Whites   99

Black Is Over (Or, Special Black)   127

The Price of Fabulousness   153

Black Girlhood, Interrupted   171

Girl 6   195

Acknowledgments   225

Notes   229

Thick

"Thick" ethnography provides readers with a proxy experience for living in another culture such that they engage with its richness, pick up the threads, and do what members do—which is to generate new meanings from the same cultural repertoire.

—Roger Gomm and Martyn Hammersley[1]

Like my women (like what?)
Thick and pretty (pretty and thick)

—Migos, "Thick & Pretty"

these hips are big hips
they need space to
move around in.
they don't fit into little
petty places. these hips
are free hips.

—Lucille Clifton

I was pregnant at thirty. Divorced at thirty-one. Lost at thirty-two. How else would I have ended up in a place called Rudean's? Rudean's was an institution. It sat in a strip mall on a street, Beatties Ford Road, that had once been the heart of the new black middle class in Charlotte, North Carolina. As went the fortunes of black homeownership, entrepreneurship, wealth creation, citizenship, and health, so went Beatties Ford Road.

Rudean's held on. So did Rudean. The establishment was named for its owner even though it perhaps would have sounded better were it not. But I do not tell old black people nothing. It is rude. What wasn't rude was Rudean's reputation. You grew up on jokes about the old players and aging fly girls living out their glory days at Rudean's, the nightclub that also sold fried fish plates and chicken wings. You had to get there early because parking was slim pickings. And there were only maybe a dozen or so tables pressed up against a long wall on the empty side of the room. The other wall had the bar, wrapped in tufted pleather and papered with liquor ads featuring smiling, glorious black people living the high life.

You ordered your fish at the bar. If you were early enough you could eat it at a table as bodies pressed by you, inching in beat together. After you ate, if you were feeling extra festive, you slid through those bodies and an oddly narrow doorway into a second room in the back. Narrow like the front room but in the different direction, horizontal to the front room's vertical, this was the dancefloor.

Going to Rudean's your first time was a rite of passage. In your teens you laughed at Rudean's. In your twenties you joked about sugar daddies at Rudean's. When you hit thirty, you busted your Rudean's cherry. On my first of only two visits to Rudean's, I sat alone at the bar waiting for friends as a man sidled up next to me. He talked, I mostly demurred and waited on my croaker plate, fried hard. Just before he asked me for my phone number he said, "Your hair thick, your nose thick, your lips thick, all of you just thick."

It was true if not artfully stated. Being too much of one thing and not enough of another had been a recurring theme in my life. I was, like many young women, expected to be small so that boys could expand and white girls could shine. When I would not or could not shrink, people made sure that I knew I had erred. I was, like many black children, too much for white teachers and white classrooms and white study groups and white Girl Scout troops and so on. Thick where I should have been thin, more when I should have been less, a high school teacher nicknamed me "Ms. Personality," and it did not feel like a superlative.

I had tried in different ways over the years to fit. I thought I could discipline my body and later my manners to take up less room. I was fine with that, but I learned that even I had limits when—in my pursuit of the life of the mind—my thinking was deemed too thick.

On one of my first forays into publishing anything, an editor told me that I was too readable to be academic, too deep to be popular, too country black to be literary, and too naive to show the rigor of my thinking in the complexity of my prose. I had wanted to create something meaningful that sounded not only like me, but like all of me. It was too thick.

Once I was at an academic conference. Well, I am at many academic conferences because I am an academic. But this conference stands out for the moment when a senior academic, a black woman, marched over to me and said without preamble, "You need to stop writing so much. They're just using you."

At the time, I was *just* a graduate student. I was finishing my dissertation, but that was not exactly the point of contention. The real point of contention was that I was also one of the most published working sociologists in print and digital media. It was and still is a strange juxtaposition.

Graduate students are not people. In the academic hierarchy, graduate students are units of labor. They can be students, but not just students. They are academics in the making. They do not have any claim to authority among scholars. In fact, the most surefire way to get a real, minted academic to speak to you when you are just a graduate student is to introduce yourself by proxy: "Hi I am Tressie, student of Richard Rubinson and Sandy Darity, and I know five other people who you recognize as people." It is hard to get that out in the three seconds humans generally give each other to establish "small talk" during routine social interactions. That is why you can, at almost any gathering of academics, find graduate students milling about in small packs, finishing sentences after someone who did this dance decades ago has already walked away.

The point that the very well-meaning senior academic was making that day was a fair one. I was not a real person. The problem was that the rest of the world did not quite know that. Or, rather, if they thought I was not a real person—one worthy of consideration and engagement—they did not think that it was because I was *just* a graduate student.

The first time anything I wrote went "viral" I was in the middle of taking exams in non-parametric statistics. It was a horrible time. The leading publication of my profession had published a hit article about a group of young scholars, almost all women of color, and all identifying as black. I wrote an essay about the article on my blog.[2] In the span of twenty-four hours the essay had become a petition that became a social media firestorm that became a series of essays on websites and blogs that became a white woman getting fired for writing the hit piece. That is as much impact as some academics have their entire lives, much less in twenty-four hours.

But the more incredible story is that I was just a black girl, a little long in the tooth, but still in my mind just a black girl writing. Black girls do not cause problems for powerful white women or august professional publications or public discourse.[3] Black girls have not, for most of my understanding of our history in this nation, had the power to cause those kinds of problems.

Black girls and black women are problems. That is not the same thing as causing problems. We are social issues to be solved, economic problems to be balanced, and emotional baggage to be overcome. We work. Lord do black girls and black women work.[4] We start work early before it is paid work. Then we start paid work and most of us never stop, are unable to ever stop. We work to keep churches financially viable,[5] black colleges in business,[6] black families functioning,[7] black politics respectable,[8] and black men alive.[9] In all of our working we can sometimes work the wrong way. That is what I was doing. I was working the wrong way . . . for a black woman who did not want to become a problem.

At the time, I was far too hurt to understand what the sister in the academic conference hall was telling me. When you are vulnerable and on the losing end of a power dynamic, all you can hear of that kind of direct, unsolicited feedback is how—despite all of your hard work—*you are still doing everything wrong*. But I have thought a lot about that moment and all the moments that have shaped what kind of thinker I have become. That is what this book is about.

Before I was a real academic, I was a black woman and before I was a black woman I was a black girl. I was a certain kind of black girl. I am the only child of an only child who was the child of a woman whose grandparents had been touched by slavery. We are southern, almost pedestrianly so.

We are the people who went north to Harlem but not west to St. Louis or California during the Great Migration when millions of black people traveled their own nation as refugees.[10] That is important to know because there is not just one black woman experience, no matter how thick one black woman may be.

My people were escaping poor white trash who made it hard to pay taxes to keep the bits of worthless land that meant the world to us to own.[11] We were escaping black men who drank too much and sometimes touched little girls too long in ways that were both wrong and acceptable. We were escaping a racial hierarchy where "injuns" could pass as biracial blacks in the shadows of Native lands that had been stolen but then cohabitated in ways that made determining who was black and who was red a game with high stakes for survival.[12] We were respectable.[13] We went to church and paid tithes and wore slips and we drank but had the good sense to be ashamed that we did. We whispered when we said bad words and we valued hard work and education as evidence of our true worth. We did not want to be problems.

Much to my chagrin I was actually born in Harlem Hospital and not a decent southern maternity ward. We were in Harlem because that is where jobs were. Shortly after I was born it became clear that my newborn chicken wings were not straightening out as nature usually demands. You know that stage when newborns are still folded up like adorable wing dings. Over time, they stretch out and develop the straight spines and legs that let us walk normal. I would not walk normally. One leg, the right one, is still clawing its way back to its in-utero comfort zone. There is a medical term for it, but we called it being pigeon-toed and bow-legged. You can be one or the other and be cute. I am both. That is not cute.

It is a kind of birth defect, really. The doctors at Harlem Hospital told my mother that it could be fixed, really should be fixed. As she tells it, the surgery would involve breaking both of my legs, resetting them, wearing hard casts and then soft, followed by however many years of braces necessary. When she tells the story, she gets a little teary-eyed. "I couldn't let them do that to my baby." And, so, I would live broken.

My mother could not fathom the cost of fixing me. But

she could count the cost of teaching me to fix myself. I have several mantras committed to memory, but the one that I remember first and most is my mother's voice shouting, "fix your feet." Every time I stood up the voice said, "fix your feet." Every time I got tired and lazy, reverting to bowed-back legs and crooked toes, it whispered, "fix your feet." When I started walking and then later started strutting, I would hear it, "fix your feet." It meant straighten your toes, adjust your hips, lock your knees, and walk like a normal person. Fixing my feet became a way of life for me, an undercurrent of thousands of messages that form the subconscious playlist of our identity. It plays alongside other whispers like, "work twice as hard" and "keep your legs closed" and "don't talk to strangers" and "don't be a stranger" and "remember who you are and where you came from."

I fixed my feet my whole life. I never walked normally, but I do not walk like I am deformed. By the time I was twelve years old the first adult man of my life told me I was sexy. "Look at her walk!" he said. The first month of my brand-new job as a professor many decades later a colleague shouted, "We knew that was you from that walk!" I had fixed my feet and they had fixed me.

Now my right hip bothers me. I have recently acquired the health insurance of the solidly middle class. To celebrate I made appointments with every kind of doctor listed in the manual. A new physical therapist brought all her colleagues around to see the extent of what they kindly call my extreme maladaptation. She tells me I should sympathize with my mother. "The science used to be so cruel, especially for children," she says. She tells me that I made it work and it is okay that after years of fixing my feet I may have worn out parts of my hip and spine. "But look how far you've come!"

I *have* come very far. I had come so far that I could be considered a problem. It is an honor of sorts. I was writing and I was doing so without express permission from gatekeepers. I had, by my third year in graduate school, published hundreds of essays in national and international newspapers and media outlets. I was called upon to weigh in on issues like technology in education, racism in higher education, social media in labor movements, and Barack Obama, period. I am now an academic, an official one. I have the job and the title and the letters after my name that black people are so fond of calling our educational credentials.

Still, there is some tension about how I got here and what I do here. I feel the tension from colleagues who cannot process why I receive so much attention. I feel it from publics who cannot fathom why I do not get more attention or different kinds of attention. Editors want me to be a journalist. Journalists want me to stay as far away from their beat as possible. Publishers want a black woman on their pages without the expense of adding one to their mastheads. No one quite knows what to make of the work that represents the intellectual journey I took from little black girl to black woman who thinks for a living.

I attribute a lot of that tension to a fundamental misunderstanding of what I do. The essays in this volume dance along the line of the dreaded "first-person essay." Dreaded because the genre has become identified with so many people and things that our culture loves to hate: women, people of color, queer people, young people, and the internet. In 2017, Jia Tolentino wrote in the *New Yorker* that the "personal-essay boom is over."[14] Tolentino was responding to a series of public articles about first-person essays in mainstream and digital publications. The first-person essay often had a hook, what we jokingly call on Twitter a "Slate pitch," named for the publication *Slate* (a Washington Post Company digital publication). A Slate pitch, or hook, is a counterintuitive headline designed to spark debate when shared on social media sites. It is often conflated with "clickbait." Clickbait are articles, content really, written for the express purpose of making people click on a link for a website that earns money from advertisers for every click it generates. A Slate pitch or counterintuitive hook is not necessarily clickbait. Very good essays are often written and then marketed using the Slate pitch. The result is all kinds of mockable headlines like "My Gynecologist Found a Ball of Cat Hair in My Vagina" that actually link to a thoughtful first-person essay about navigating societal expectations of cleanliness as a woman.[15]

Regardless, the rush for advertising dollars that had fueled the personal essay was over. The epilogues had been written. They went something like this: women writers had oversaturated a market with their self-indulgent essays about issues that cannot scale to a general audience. These women writers had done so mostly for pay but more so for attention, as there was very little good pay happening for the personal essay. Predatory publications used these women to drive their internet traffic, subjecting them to ridicule and even real violence when nefarious groups targeted these writers for harassment. The personal essay was dead and not a minute too soon.

Except the personal essay dragnet may have been cast too wide and too deep to be of much use as a device for anything but systemic discrimination. Black women writers spoke up about the personal essay. For them, it was the only point of access for telling the creative stories of empirical realities. Latinas said the same. Queer women and trans women and all manner of women stepped forward to add dimensions to what the personal essay form is and what it is assumed to be.

The personal essay was an economic problem and a social problem dressed up as a cultural taste problem. The woman with cat hair in her vagina is probably certifiably insane.

Let's just get that out of the way. I do not ever want to know about that much cat hair being in any bodily orifice. I am also anti-cat, generally speaking, and definitely when the issue is fur balls in one's vaginal cavity. I do not want to read it. I also do not want to read about men's fascination with guns or stock car racing or long walks in the woods. I do not want to read *Infinite Jest* or talk to people about reading *Infinite Jest*. I do not want to listen to stories about Lake Wobegon or the mild humor of white suburban interpersonal politics. None of those things appeal to me and yet all of these takes on the personal essay were excluded from the form's obituary. We weren't killing the personal essay so much as were killing those who used the personal essay to become a problem.

The obituaries missed this because their authors do not know about fixing their feet. That is a black woman's specialty. The personal essay had become the way that black women writers claim legitimacy in a public discourse that defines itself, in part, by how well it excludes black women. In a modern society, who is allowed to speak with authority is a political act. Of course, all U.S. citizens are allowed to speak. We have an entire amendment guaranteeing us this right with notable exclusions like hate speech and prisoners, who can be arbitrarily denied speech by the State. But not all of us are presumed by the publics to which we belong to have the right to speak authoritatively. Speech becomes rhetoric, or a persuasive form of speech, only when the one speaking can make a legitimate claim to some form of authority. It can be moral authority or legal authority or rational authority. At every turn, black women have been categorically excluded from being expert performers of persuasive speech acts in the public that adjudicates our humanity.

As women, black women face challenges of appealing to rationality in public discourse because our culture has decided that women are irrational and emotional. Logic and reason are beyond our biological and cultural programming. Excluded from the discourse that is ruled by what I have called Professionally Smart People, or those who are institutionalized as the official rational voices in public rhetoric, black women could try to appeal to their moral authority. In a modern capitalist society, what is moral is often determined by what has economic value.[16]

As social and economic subjects in this system, we ad hoc ascribe morality to all kinds of capital and status that reifies social categories that exclude black women by definition: wealth, high income, professional status, marriageability, religious leadership, beauty. The very moral goods that would suffice to make moral claims in public discourse are delimited by how efficiently they do not include black women. Empirically, black women have generations of earned and inherited moral philosophy that has sustained families, communities, and institutions. Despite this, black women find that the public discourse is not generally willing to accept that we are moral authorities on much at all.

Where black women have excelled is in the pursuit of legal authority, or the technical qualifications of social status. We go to school. We will, on average, go to all the school that the constraints on our time and money will allow us. Black women have high educational aspirations and continue to outflank black men in educational attainment. Even outside that narrow purview of professionalization, though, black women strive for forms of professional status. We start businesses at surprisingly high rates given how little family wealth we have to draw on or social networks we have to support us. We perform phenomenally high rates of community service and lay leadership in churches, schools, and civic organizations. We are, it could be argued, professional professionals. In public discourse, our aspirations and achievements in professions should translate into the right to speak authoritatively on *something*. On anything. On politics. On economics. On sports. On education. On climate science. On urbanization. At the very least on our own lives.

But, as Stacia L. Brown points out in her essay on how and why black women writers find themselves hewn to the personal essay genre, black women find that no amount of pathos, logos, or ethos includes them in the civic sphere of public discourse and persuasion. We do not have enough authority, as judged by the audiences and gatekeepers who decide to whom we should listen, to speak on much of anything.[17] For us, the personal essay genre became a contested point of entry into a low-margin form of public discourse where we could at least appeal to the politics of white feminist inclusion for nominal representation. We were writing personal essays because as far as authoritative voices go, the self was the only subject men and white people would cede to us.

We had learned or have always known that we cannot change the public, and we cannot change the minds of those on whom we rely to grant us the audience that confers moral authority to speak in public. We could not fix the world but we could fix our own feet. And so, black women writers have fixed their feet. We have shoehorned political analysis and economic policy and social movements theory and queer ideologies into public discourse by bleeding our personal lives into the genre afforded us.

Legacy media and majority-white-owned digital media platforms made more money from black women's personal essays than any black woman I know of ever made from publishing them. That is what the senior academic meant when she said they were using me. She thought that the *Washington Post* and *Slate* (where I had a column for a while) and *Dissent* and *Talking Points Memo* and *The Atlantic* and the other twenty-plus outlets that had published my essays were using me to darken their web hits without darkening their staff. I was bleeding when I should have been thinking. Thinking was the job of a graduate student, not bleeding.

The problem for me was not the second part of the sister's proclamation, but the first: stop writing. I can no more stop writing than I can stop fixing my feet. It is killing my hip and it may look sexy to a subset of geriatric black men who like their women thicker than a snicker, but I cannot stop executing my extreme maladaptation. Fixing my feet is so deeply ingrained in my psyche that to dislodge it I would have to fundamentally change who I am and how I interact with the world. Fixing my feet is about accepting the complex reality of black life in the twenty-first century. I am living in the most opportune time in black history in the United States and that means, still, that I will die younger, live poorer, risk more exposure to police violence, and be punished by social policy for being a black woman in ways that aren't true for almost any other group in this nation. That is the best it has ever been to be black in America and it is still that statistically bad at the macro level.

Fixing my feet means knowing that I am no one's beauty queen and few people's idea of an intellectual, public or otherwise, and showing up anyway. Fixing my feet means knowing how badly the outcomes are likely to be for persisting and pursuing, but doing it anyway. I fix myself, even when it causes great pain to do so, because I know that I cannot fix the way the world sees me.

When I write, I am fixing my feet. I am claiming the ethos, or moral authority, to influence public discourse. And I am defying every expectation when I do it. What I am not doing is writing personal essays. Despite knowing how critical the genre is to black women's participation in publics, I cannot in good faith say that I have ever thought of my essays as belonging to the genre. At the same time, I am not one of the literary writers of black experience. I do not paint ethereal black worlds where white people can slip into our narratives and leave unscathed by judgment for their unearned privilege. I am also not that kind of beautiful writer that I love—the ones who tell the stories that arrive in my issue of the *Oxford American* every quarter. Those glorious artists who win awards at programs where they wear flowy dresses and take pictures mid–sanguine smile.

I am hopelessly tethered to reality, not fiction or even

creative nonfiction. I may be a storyteller, but even that is more a claim of birthright than any legitimate claim that I can make to the craft of telling stories. I am not even, perhaps, a stodgy sociologist or cut-and-dried ethnographer. My ethnographies have too much structure and my sociology is a bit too loose with voice. A bit slutty it all is, really, jumping between forms and disciplines and audiences. My writing has a high body count, as the kids say.

But sociology comes as close to the core of where my essays start as anything else I have explored. Drawing on what ethnographers have called thick description, I finally found a label as complex as my way of thinking. I take very seriously the idea of social locations. We are people, with free will, circumscribed to different degrees by histories that shape who we are allowed to become. I am, by most measures, pretty smart. My grandmother was smarter. She was do-the-*Times*-crossword-in-pen smart. She was teach-yourself-liberal-arts-with-a-library-card smart. She was, for most of her life, a domestic worker for rich Jewish people who sent me cards when I got good grades in school. The Edelmans. The Goldmans. The Finkelsteins.

When she died, quickly, thank God, all of my grandmother's possessions fit inside the one-bedroom senior living apartment in the small town where she had been born. She was far smarter than her Ph.D.-having granddaughter and she died poor. Smart is only a construct of correspondence, between one's abilities, one's environment, and one's moment in history. I am smart in the right way, in the right time, on the right end of globalization.

That's where my essays always begin, by interrogating why me and not my grandmother? Why now and not then? Why this U.S. and not some other U.S.? What, more simply, does my social location say about our society? That is quite different from trying to figure out how everything in our society is about me. My experience cannot speak to immigration, for example. It cannot speak to lesbian or gay or queer lives. A personal essay would not make the distinction. That is not a diss. It is a difference.

By interrogating my social location with a careful eye on thick description that moves between empirics and narrative, I have—over the course of hundreds of essays and more than a decade of public writing for an audience who recognized me as a voice of some kind—tried to explore what our selves say about our society. Along the way, I have shared parts of myself, my history, and my identity to make social theory concrete. The things we touch and smell and see and experience through our senses are how stories become powerful. But I have never wanted to only tell powerfully evocative stories. I have wanted to tell evocative stories that become a problem for power. For that, I draw upon data and research.

In every essay in this collection there is a wealth of theory and data, some academic and some lived, some primary and some secondary, informing every detail of my argument. And these are arguments, in the philosophical sense. They are written to persuade, to change, to effect. That is why who I am matters all the more and not less. Excluded as I am from the ethos, logos, and pathos of academia, literary arts, humanities, and Professional Smart People, I have had to appeal to every form of authority simultaneously in every single thing that I have ever written. It is how I fix my feet.

Unfortunately, I may have been too good at fixing my feet. Often the work of the argument has been challenged, gone unnoticed, or, at least, uncommented upon. That is why versions of some of my previous essays are included here, but this time I am showing my work to make clear the thinking that informed them. An essay about Miley Cyrus pantomiming sex acts on MTV is really about the libidinal economy that, ironically enough, shapes the personal essay economy that made that essay famous. Comedian Leslie Jones's performance of vulnerability on *Saturday Night Live* is about colorism and colonialism. Few things shaped my essay on how and why poor people make certain purchases instead of saving money as much as thinking about Veblen, Bourdieu, and black literature from the mid-twentieth century.

Longtime readers of my work may recognize some parts of these essays, but will find that each of them has been rewritten. My thinking is not fixed in time and hopefully it never will be. I become more radical about some things as I get older. I am also more forgiving of pettiness these days even as I become intolerant of willful ignorance. I have fourteen reading spots in my home and three in my university office. I read on a Kindle and the Kindle app on my

Google phone and with library apps like Overdrive. I have twenty-nine alerts set up for online scholarly databases. Those alerts send me new research featuring my keywords whenever they are published. I buy more periodicals than I will ever fully consume. I read and think a lot. To the extent possible, my entire life is organized to find me fifteen more minutes every day in which I can read slowly, often using my finger as I did as a child, across new words and new ideas. If any of my essays could be republished without rewriting them, I would have failed as the human I work diligently to be.

Those spaces to read are a privilege. I have not a room of my own, but a whole house. Occasionally I am asked to hold forth on being a woman academic. Then, as now, I am always clear that I am an exception to many rules. I do not have children or a spouse. I am not yet a full-time caregiver for my parents. I do not come from money. I am, in many ways, the people I study. I have six-figure student loan debt, did not have a credit card that could buy an airline ticket until maybe three years ago, and I obsessively hoard loose change so that I can at least have more than the roughly

$300 in the bank that the typical black woman in the United States does not have in savings. Still, I am high-earning. I may work five jobs to afford it, but I can, on occasion, pay a student to edit a paper or an on-demand worker to deliver my groceries. With the privilege to read and to think comes great responsibility. When you have that privilege precisely because so many others like you—black women—are systematically filtered out of every level of social status, then the responsibility is especially great.

I hope these essays break open space for black women thinkers to do what we are already doing but for better rewards. As I have said to anyone who will listen to me, I want a black woman to have one damn job and not five or six. In fact, I want that for all of us; job guarantees and universal basic incomes are part of my core political beliefs. But I would be lying if I said that I did not want that kind of baseline economic security first and most of all for sisters. These essays are part of how I came to many of my core beliefs, complete with the privileges to think, the struggle of working multiple jobs to afford those privileges, and the moral philosophy derived from fixing my feet.

———

If anyone ever reads me and finds it useful, as I hope that you do, may doing so spark a gold rush for black women writers at institutions and publications that will pay them and protect them. I hope we build a body politic so thick with contradictions and nuance and humanity and blackness (because blackness is humanity), that no black woman public intellectual has to fix her feet ever again to walk this world.

In the Name of Beauty

We need to theorize the meaning of beauty in our lives so that we can educate for critical consciousness, talking through the issues: how we acquire and spend money, how we feel about beauty, what the place of beauty is in our lives when we lack material privilege and even basic resources for living, the meaning and significance of luxury, and the politics of envy.

—bell hooks[1]

[T]he very lifestyle of the holders of power contributes to the power that makes it possible, because its true conditions of possibility remain unrecognized.

—Pierre Bourdieu[2]

Miley Cyrus was going through her dangerous phase. She had tattoos and piercings and dildos and so, of course, she also had to have some black affect to complete the package. It is all part of the pop star toolkit. I decided to write about it. Now, it is pretty common for people, sometimes lots of them, to respond to things I write. Sometimes they share heartbreaking stories of recognition. Other times, angry diatribes about what I get wrong while being black, a woman, and popular. But of all the things I have written, nothing has inspired more direct, intense emotional engagement than what I wrote about post-Disney pop star Miley Cyrus. What had me stuck—momentarily—wasn't just the heightened emotions of those who took me to task, but rather who was leading the charge.

I am accustomed to men and white people being angry with me. That is par for the course. But when black women are mad at me it is a special kind of contrition, and I take the time to figure out my responsibility. Something clearly wasn't registering in this scenario, because black women were giving me the business.[3]

Sisters weren't really angry about my breakdown of just how dangerous Miley Cyrus's performance on a televised award show actually was. They weren't exactly angry that I pointed out the size and shape of the black woman dancers behind her. What many black women were angry about was how I located myself in what I'd written. I said, blithely as a matter of observable fact, that I am unattractive. Because I am unattractive, the argument went, I have a particular kind of experience of beauty, race, racism, and interacting with what we might call the white gaze. I thought nothing of it at the time I was writing it, which is unusual. I can usually pinpoint what I have said, written, or done that will piss people off and which people will be pissed off. I missed this one entirely.

The comments were brutal and feedback wasn't confined to the internet. Things got personal. One black male colleague emailed me to say how a black woman friend told him she did not want to read some trash article about how ugly I am when my accompanying picture belied the claim. It was, she insinuated, an appeal for public validation of my physical attractiveness. I did not think that was true, but I was raised right. I told him that was fair and drank myself to sleep. Someone else sent me a link to a Facebook group where many women, but especially more than a few black women, took me to task for hating myself. The person who sent it did not know that I was already a member of the group and had been watching the carnage for days. I never mentioned it.

A few months after the essay had been published, I was scheduled to deliver the Mason Sankora Lecture for the Department of English at my alma mater, a historically black college. It was a brutal experience because an HBCU is a special place. I am not the first to acknowledge that, of course.[4] You can learn all about the legacy, the culture, the challenges, and the faults of black colleges in books, articles, movies, television shows, and documentaries. But few of those things have ever described the primary reason why HBCUs are so special to me.

When I was eleven years old, my waist caved in and my breasts sprung out. I could not be left alone at the school bus stop anymore. It was dangerous because men can be dangerous. I had some preparation for that. My mother had been, I believe, sexually victimized as a child. She doesn't speak of it except when her sentences fade out in retelling certain stories. But it was there in how protective she was of me, an only child of a single mother. There were no men allowed in our house except for family and even then only under her direct guidance. "I wanted your home to be safe, made for children and not adults," she has told me. Only children learn to gauge their single parent's emotional needs. It is vital for your survival and, you eventually learn, necessary if you are going to help your only adult protection in the world keep you both safe. I intuited from my mother's caution that I should be cautious of men, defensive of whatever I was calling home at any given time—my heart, my mental health, my car, my bedroom, my checkbook, my dreams, my body. Decades before I valued myself enough to be careful for myself, I was careful so that my mother would not worry.

If I knew to be cautious of men, I did not learn early enough to be cautious of white women. The first time a white woman teacher told me that my breasts were distracting was in the sixth grade. Over the years, white women with authority over me have told me how wrong or dangerous or deviant my body is. As with that teacher, many of their comments focus on my breasts as opposed to, say, my ass. The next year I entered middle school, where you learn the rules of sexual presentation. That is where I started to discover that while my breasts distracted some of the boys and men, all distractions were not created equally.

As part of the last generation of Carolinians to attend the integrated schools that *Brown v. Board of Education* ushered into existence, I went to school with a lot of white people. Because of the racial composition of the districts drawn in my then-progressive school district, I also went to school with many South Asian and Latino kids. That racial and ethnic integration mattered to the rules I learned about being sexual, desirable, visible, and unseen.

Unlike home, where much of my social world was filtered through my mother's preference for African American history and culture, at school I learned that nothing was more beautiful than blond. The first time it happened was middle school. I heard a white boy, a bit of a loser with a crooked haircut who acted out because he couldn't bear to be unseen, say "that's a real blonde" about a girl in class, and I was confused. The only hair coloring I knew of at fourteen years old was the kind my grandmother used to "fix her edges," where curly gray hairs did not blend in properly with her wig. I had no idea what a "real" or "fake" blonde was, but I could intuit, much like my mother's fears, that the slacker boy was communicating some valuable social fact.

Later, we watched the musical *Grease* in a high school English class. In the final scene, when Olivia Newton John's Sandy shows up at the carnival in shiny skin-tight pants, all the black kids tittered. She looked funny! There was so much space between her legs! A white boy too tall to be in the tenth grade reared back and shouted, "My hot damn, Ms. Newton John!" I remember the scene so clearly, because that was when I got it. A whole other culture of desirability had been playing out just above and beyond my awareness, while my mostly black and Latino friends traded jokes at gapped thighs, flat behinds, and never trusting a big butt and a smile. And when the teacher, a middle-aged white woman not unlike the one who once told me my breasts were too distracting, looked at the too-tall boy, she smiled at him and rolled her eyes, acknowledging his sexual appreciation of Sandy as normal if unmannerly. He smiled back and kind of shrugged as if to say, "I just can't help myself." The teacher and the too-tall boy were in cahoots. Sandy, that strange creature, was *beautiful*.

Middle school moments—school dances and lunchroom strategies and weekend sleepovers—start to shake out the racial segregation of even the most utopian integrated schools. The white kids were your school friends, never your home friends. You took the gifted math classes together but you would not be on the lake with them over the weekend. We took that as normal. When we were together, politely sociable in classrooms and hallways, I learned what was beautiful. By high school, I knew that I was not it.

All girls in high school have self-esteem issues. And most girls compare themselves to unattainable, unrealistic physical ideals. That is not what I am talking about. That is the violence of gender that happens to all of us in slightly different ways. I am talking about a kind of capital. It is not just the preferences of a too-tall boy, but the way authority validates his preferences as normal. I had high school boyfriends. I had a social circle. I had evidence that I was valuable in certain contexts. But I had also parsed that there was something powerful about blondness, thinness, flatness, and gaps between thighs. And that power was the context against which all others defined themselves. That was beauty. And while few young women in high school could say they felt like they lived up to beauty, only the non-white girls could never be beautiful. That is because beauty isn't actually what you look like; beauty is the preferences that reproduce the existing social order. What is beautiful is whatever will keep weekend lake parties safe from strange darker people.

When white feminists catalogue how beauty standards over time have changed, from the "curvier" Marilyn Monroe to the skeletal Twiggy to the synthetic-athletic Pamela Anderson, their archetypes belie beauty's true function: whiteness. Whiteness exists as a response to blackness.

Whiteness is a violent sociocultural regime legitimized by property to always make clear who is black by fastidiously delineating who is officially white. It would stand to reason that beauty's ultimate function is to exclude blackness. That beauty also violently conditions white women and symbolically precludes the existence of gender nonconforming people is a bonus. Some of the white girls I went to high school with may not have been beautiful. They may be thin when they should be fit or narrow of jaw when it should be strong. But, should power need them to be, social, economic, and political forces could make those girls beautiful by reshaping social norms. As long as the beautiful people are white, what is beautiful at any given time can be renegotiated without redistributing capital from white to nonwhite people.

Feminists have chronicled the changing standards of female beauty over time. One of the more popular examples of this is reborn on the internet every couple of years. In the meme, readers are asked to guess what size dress Marilyn Monroe would wear today. One is supposed to gasp at the realization that the iconic popular culture beauty was a *size twelve*. Memes are just born-digital nuggets of cultural norms.[5] Whether the LOLcat is funny or Marilyn is beautiful or a gif of a YouTube prank is gross all depends on the norms of the culture that produced the meme.[6] In the case of Marilyn Monroe's dress size, the meme assumes a western U.S. iconography. Marilyn is not just beautiful; she defines the beauty ideals of an entire era in U.S. popular culture. If you do not recognize that belief as your own, the meme will make no sense. The expectation that you should be shocked by Marilyn's dress size also relies on an audience who will share an idea about who is fat. And the audience must share the notion that fat and beauty are antithetical. Of course, fat has not always been juxtaposed against beauty in white western culture. Artists point to the Rubenesque female bodies of the seventeenth century as an example of how fat bodies were once the beauty ideal. They are also an ideal meant to lionize a version of white western history.

Naomi Wolf made the idea of examining beauty ideals across time a white third wave feminist cause du jour. In *The Beauty Myth*, Wolf excises the expectations of female beauty from the economic context that produces them, holding both up for feminist critique.[7] As others have noted, Wolf does not do much work on how economic and political conditions produce a white hegemonic body as the ultimate expression of beauty.[8] More precisely, Wolf demonstrates that as the sociopolitical context of whiteness—the political, state-sanctioned regime—tussles with historical forces like falling stock markets, mass media, suburbanization, and war, it will reshape an acceptable beauty standard for women that adjusts for body types, but never for body color. That was not Wolf's argument, but the absence of such a critique rather proves the point: beauty is for white women.[9] It is a white woman's problem, if you are a feminist, or a white woman's grace, if you are something else not feminist. Beauty, in a meme or in the beauty myth, only holds as a meaningful cultural artifact through which we can examine politics, economics, and laws, and identity if we all share the assumption that beauty *is* precisely *because* it excludes nonwhite women.

Black women have examined where we are located in the beauty myth, examining the political economy through our bodies. If we could never be assumed beautiful in white culture's memes, histories, and feminisms, we could create other standards. Like feminist critiques of Rubens's renderings of white jiggling flesh, we have turned to cultural production for evidence of how we can ever be beautiful. Patricia Hill Collins's *Black Sexual Politics* is the most notable shot across the bow.[10] Collins does not exactly wade into the complicated depth of race, class, nationalism, culture, economics, and the politics of how black sexuality is refracted through the racial hierarchy that precludes black women from being beautiful. She is, however, critical to defining a school of intellectual thought that gives us tools to understand these dynamics. Some of her most strident critique is saved for the compromises inherent in hip-hop culture. Here is a cultural product where blackness can be a critical feedback loop to the white mass media images of black women as caricatures. What Collins finds instead is a space where black masculine ideas about black women create ever more hierarchies of desirability based on body type, for example. Those hierarchies rarely go so far as to challenge the supremacy of white female beauty.

Black hip-hop feminists brought a deeper engagement with the complexities of hip-hop culture to bear on Collins's critique. Joan Morgan's *When Chickenheads Come Home to Roost: A Hip-Hop Feminist Breaks It Down* locates a black feminist voice in hip-hop culture, however marginalized in mainstream media.[11] Despite arguing that the generation I claim is "misguidedly over-protective, hopelessly male-identified, and all too often self-sacrificing," hip-hop era feminists excavate a cultural history where we have tried to claim a space for black beauty. In 2014, comedian Leslie Jones performed a skit on *Saturday Night Live* about the complexities of claiming that space.[12] In the skit, she turns the pain of racist beauty hierarchies that academics on the order of Marcus Hunter have studied into the kind of joke that made Richard Pryor so great. For approximately three minutes Jones bemoans her singleness. It is a frequent well from which she draws in her comedy. The topic is the designation of Lupita N'yongo as *People's* Most Beautiful Woman. Jones says that she is "waiting for them to put out the Most Useful List because that's where I'm gonna shine." It is a painful comment but not unfathomable given what beauty means, even if it said to be embodied by dark-skinned Kenyan-Mexican actress Nyong'o.

Jones is flatly saying that she is not beautiful and cannot be beautiful but that she is useful. She is locating her value not in beauty but in her use value. The real criticism was directed at her turn to slavery: "back in the slave days I would've never been single. I am six feet tall and I am strong! I'm just saying back in the slave days my love life would have been way better. Massa would've hooked me up with the best brother on the plantation." It hurts to watch the video. It's the kind of humor located in pain, not unlike that mined by Richard Pryor a generation ago. But we allowed Pryor his pain. He was an addict with self-esteem issues. He could set himself on fire and turn "nigga" into an incantation, often for white audiences. But Jones was not allowed to talk about the pain of being undesirable.

Free but black in the white western beauty myth, Jones is laying bare how futile it can be to desire beauty as a black woman. Many people slammed Jones for making light of slavery, especially of the systematic rape of enslaved black women. The argument was that she was mining historical pain for white consumption on a program that its creator Lorne Michaels once intoned would never be an "urban" show. I recall watching the skit and the ensuing social media firestorm about it with dismay. Not a single black woman that I read or followed seemed to empathize with Jones's obvious pain, whereas I had not been able to watch the video clip without pausing several times. Where others saw insult, I saw injury. The joke was not on enslaved black women of yesteryear but on the idea that it would take a totalizing system of enslavement to counter the structural violence that beauty does to Jones in her life today. Perhaps I caught what others missed because I am something different than Patricia Hill Collins or Joan Morgan or other important black women scholars of black feminism.

I am dark, physically and culturally. My complexion is not close to whiteness and my family roots reflect the economic realities of generations of dark-complexioned black people. We are rural, even when we move to cities. Our mobility is modest. Our out-marriage rates to nonblack men are negligible. Our social networks do not connect to elite black social institutions. When we move around in the world, we brush up against the criminal justice system. I am not located at the top of hip-hop's attenuated beauty hierarchy. I am, at best, in the middle. As Michael Jackson once sang, when you're too high to get over it and too low to get under it, you are stuck in the middle and the pain is thunder.

We have yet to make strides toward fleshing out a theory of desirability, the desire to be desired, in black feminist theory or politics. There is indeed a philosophy in how Jones desires being desired. That Nyong'o was atop a list of the world's most beautiful people does not invalidate the reality for many dark-skinned black women any more than Mark Zuckerburg making a billion dollars as a college drop-out invalidates the value of college for millions. Indeed, any system of oppression must allow exceptions to validate itself as meritorious. How else will those who are oppressed by the system internalize their own oppression? This is what I did not yet understand that when I was watching Ms. Newton John: I was not beautiful and could never—no matter what was in fashion to serve the interests of capital and power—become beautiful. That was the theory trapped in my bones when I left for my mecca, my HBCU.

My first night as a college freshman at my HBCU, I ordered a pizza. The man-boy who delivered it stared too long before he handed it over. I snapped and grabbed my pizza. As I did, he muttered something about my phone number. I would date him off and on for a decade. As I walked back into the lobby of Eagleson Hall, I turned just as the pizza man-boy caught the eye of our dorm supervisor, an older black man. The man gave him a look like the one the teacher had once given the too-tall boy overtaken by Olivia Newton John's spandexed thighs. I was Sandy!

At this institution I could be a kind of beautiful: normal, normative, taken for granted as desirable. It is one of many reasons that I loved my HBCU. Not because I got a few phone numbers or had a few boyfriends, but because I wasn't being defined by a standard of beauty that, by definition, could not include someone who looked like me. Don't get me wrong, the standard is complicated. It has the same economic costs to perform it as the ones white feminists argue that the massive global beauty industry exacts from white women. The costs may be even higher, because black women have fewer resources to purchase the accoutrements of thin waists, thick hips, tattooed brows, elegant contouring, red-heeled shoes, and femme styling that contemporary black beauty

standards require. Black women experience negative consequences for not performing it sufficiently, especially if they
are not straight, cisgender, and otherwise normative. But,
feeling desired opened up avenues of inclusion that shaped
my sense of self.

That inclusion is what I was coming home to the day I
delivered a lecture at my dear ol' NCC. After sixty minutes
or so of talking about the things my hosts had asked me to
discuss, I opened the floor to questions. The first one was
from a young sister about halfway back and to my left. The
lighting shadowed her face, but I could make out her body
language. I speak black woman fluently. My body recognized hers and I stood up straighter as she took the micro-
phone and said, "We read your thing in class and Miley
Cyrus ain't even do all that. Just because you ugly don't
mean all black women are ugly." The room lit up. It seems
all the English professors in attendance had assigned that
essay as an example of what I do. And everyone in attendance had thoughts and feelings about it.

I did a little verbal dancing, trying to explain how we
critique popular culture, and then moved on to the next

question. Another young woman, another comment on how black and white people are friends now, unlike back in the day. Those black women are Miley's friends—and the white women I have written about who touch me in public are apparently doing so because they want to be my friend. Again, the idea of my body's value in social contexts was the a priori issue. These students were saying, in as many ways as they could, that I could not be ugly because white people find me desirable.

They were also saying, in their insistence and with their bodies, what more seasoned black women were saying to me in response to my essay. They were saying we had fought too long, worked too hard, come too far to concede that what white people have said about us is true. White people, as a collective system of cultural and economic production that has colonized nonwhite people across the globe through military and ideological warfare, have said that black people are animalistic. But, as sister bell hooks and many others have pointed out, animals with dicks can be useful. They can be "tall, dark, and handsome" if not also dangerous. There is no ideological exception to anti-blackness for black women but through colorism. Mulatto, "mixed," high yellow, light—all euphemisms for black people whose phenotype signals that they may have some genetic proximity to whiteness. But, by definition, black women are not beautiful except for any whiteness that may be in them.

Black women have worked hard to write a counternarrative of our worth in a global system where beauty is the only legitimate capital allowed women without legal, political, and economic challenge. That last bit is important. Beauty is not *good* capital. It compounds the oppression of gender. It constrains those who identify as women against their will. It costs money and demands money. It colonizes. It hurts. It is painful. It can never be fully satisfied. It is not useful for human flourishing. Beauty is, like all capital, merely valuable.[13]

Because it is valuable, black women have said that we are beautiful too. We have traveled the cultural imaginations of the world's nonwhite people assembling a beauty construct that does not exclude us. We create culture about our beauty. We negotiate with black men to legitimize our beauty. We try to construct something that feels like liberation in an inherently oppressive regime, balancing peace with our marginally more privileged lighter-skinned black women while refuting the global caste status of darker-skinned black women. Some of us try to include multiple genders and politics in our definition of beauty. This kind of work requires discursive loyalty. We must name it and claim it, because naming is about the only unilateral power we have.

When I say that I am unattractive, concede that I am ugly, the antithesis of beauty, I sound like I am internalizing a white standard of beauty that black women fight hard to rise above. But my truth is quite the opposite. When oppressed people become complicit in their oppression, joining the dominant class in their ideas about what we are, it is symbolic violence. Like all concepts, symbolic violence has a context that is important for using it to mean what we intend to mean. It is not just that internalizing the values of the dominant class violently stigmatizes us. Symbolic violence only makes sense if we accept its priors: all preferences in imperial, industrialized societies are shaped by the economic system. There aren't any "good" preferences. There are only preferences that are validated by others, differently, based on social contexts.

These contexts should not just be reduced to race, class, and gender, as important as those are. Institutions that legitimize the "right" ideas and behaviors also matter. That's why beauty can never be about preference. "I just like what I like" is always a capitalist lie. Beauty would be a useless concept for capital if it were only a preference in the purest sense. Capital demands that beauty be coercive. If beauty matters at all to how people perceive you, how institutions treat you, which rules are applied to you, and what choices you can make, then beauty must also be a structure of patterns, institutions, and exchanges that eats your preferences for lunch.

Internalizing your inferiority is violent. Psychologically it cleaves you in two, what W.E.B. DuBois famously called the double veil. As our science becomes more advanced, we find that the violence may even show up in our bodies as stress. Structurally, that violence becomes coded in the social norms around respectability that we black people use to do the dominant culture's work of disciplining other black people's identities, behaviors, and bodies. It is rational to check me if I am doing this kind of work for the devil.

But lest we forget, the greatest trick the devil ever pulled was convincing us that he does not exist. That is why naming is political. Our so-called counternarratives about beauty and what they demand of us cannot be divorced from the fact that beauty is contingent upon capitalism. Even our resistance becomes a means to commodify, and what is commodified is always, always stratified. There is simply no other way. To coerce, beauty must exclude. Exclusion can be part of a certain kind of liberation, where one dominant regime is overthrown for another, but it cannot be universal.

I love us loving ourselves under the most difficult conditions, but I must also write into my idea of truth and freedom. From my perch, trying to fillet the thinnest sections of popular culture, history, sociology, and my own biography, there isn't any room for error. I have to call a thing a thing. And sometimes, when we are trapped in the race not to be complicit in our own oppression, self-definition masquerades as a notion of loving our black selves in white terms. More than that, critique that hides the power being played out in the theater of our everyday lives only serves that power. It doesn't actually challenge it.

When I say that I am unattractive or ugly, I am not internalizing the dominant culture's assessment of me. I am naming what has been done to me. And signaling who did it.

I am glad that doing so unsettles folks, including the many white women who wrote to me with impassioned cases for how beautiful I am. They offered me neoliberal self-help nonsense that borders on the religious. They need me to believe beauty is both achievable and individual, because the alternative makes them vulnerable. If you did not earn beauty, never had the real power to reject it, then you are as much a vulnerable subject as I am in your own way. Deal with that rather than dealing with me. Compared with the forms of oppression they can now see via their proximity to me, it may seem to privileged people that it is easier to fix me than it is to fix the world. I live to disabuse people of that notion.

But it is interesting to think about why many white women, a handful of white men, and a few black men rejected my claim. Their interests cannot be the same as those of black women, whose stake in my claim that beauty excludes me is deeply intimate.

White women, especially white feminists, need me to lean in to pseudoreligious consumerist teachings that beauty is democratic and achievable. Beauty must be democratic. If it is not, then beauty becomes a commodity, distributed unequally and, even worse, at random. This is a notion often ascribed to a type of feminism, be it neoliberal feminism, marketplace feminism, or consumption feminism. But well-meaning white women also need me to believe because accessing beauty is about the totalizing construct of gender, in this case femininity, in a world where other forms of lifestyle consumption are splintering.

You can use an app to buy the foods of the rich, the music of the cool, the art of the revolutionary, and the look of the aspirational. But femininity is resistant to appification and frictionless consumption. Femininity is not about biological sex, but about the traits that have become ascribed to biological sex. And this set of traits carries a set of ideas and histories contingent upon the economics and politics of any given time. You cannot separate what it means to be a "woman," often used to mean a performance of acceptable femininity, from the conditions that decide what is and is not acceptable across time and space. We all do this kind of performance of ourselves, be it our gender or race or social class or national identity or culture. As we are doing it, we are always negotiating with powerful ideas about what constitutes a woman.

Beauty has an aesthetic, but it is not the same as aesthetics, not when it can be embodied, controlled by powerful interests, and when it can be commodified. Beauty can be manners, also a socially contingent set of traits. Whatever power decides that beauty is, it must always be more than reducible to a single thing. Beauty is a wonderful form of capital in a world that organizes everything around gender and then requires a performance of gender that makes some of its members more equal than others.

Beauty would not be such a useful distinction were it not for the economic and political conditions. It is trite at this point to point out capitalism, which is precisely why it must be pointed out. Systems of exchange tend to generate the kind of ideas that work well as exchanges. Because it can be an idea *and* a good *and* a body, beauty serves many useful functions for our economic system. Even better, beauty can be political. It can exclude and include, one of the basic conditions of any politics. Beauty has it all. It can be political, economic, external, individualized, generalizing, exclusionary, and perhaps best of all a story that can be told. Our dominant story of beauty is that it is simultaneously a blessing, of genetics or gods, and a site of conversion. You can *become* beautiful if you accept the right prophets and their wisdoms with a side of products thrown in for good measure. Forget that these two ideas—unique blessing and earned reward—are antithetical to each other. That makes beauty all the more perfect for our (social and political) time, itself anchored in paradoxes like freedom *and* property, opportunity *and* equality.[14]

There is now an entire shelf among the periodicals at my nearby chain bookstore filled with magazines that will give me five meditations or three coloring book pages or nine yoga retreats or fourteen farmhouse ideas or nineteen paper-crafting inspirations that, if purchased, will acculturate me to achievable "inner beauty." Mind you, the consumption is always external and public. These are quite literally called "lifestyle" magazines, which begs the question "Whose life-style?" These are ways of expressing a kind of femininity, a kind of woman, for whom beauty is defined to selectively include or exclude. These are consumption goods made for a lifestyle associated with white western women of a certain status, class, profession, and disposition. These are for women who *can* be beautiful, if only conditionally, and contingent upon the needs of markets and states—and the men whom states and markets serve most and best. All of the admonishments that I should "love myself" and am "as cute as a button" from well-intentioned white women stem from their need for me to consume what is produced for them.

What those white women did not know or could not admit to knowing is that I cannot, by definition, ever be that kind of beautiful. In the way that gender has so structured how we move through the intersecting planes of class and status and income and wealth that shape our world and our selves, so does race. Rather, I should say, so does blackness, because everyone—including white women— have "race." It is actually blackness, as it has been created through the history of colonization, imperialism, and domination, that excludes me from the forces of beauty. For beauty to function as it should, it must exclude me. Big Beauty—the structure of who can be beautiful, the stories we tell about beauty, the value we assign beauty, the power given to those with beauty, the disciplining effect of the fear of losing beauty you might possess—definitionally excludes the kind of blackness I carry in my history and my bones. Beauty is for white women, if not for all white women. If beauty is to matter at all for capital, it can never be for black women.

But if I *believe* that I can become beautiful, I become an economic subject. My desire becomes a market. And my faith becomes a salve for the white women who want to have the right politics while keeping the privilege of never having to live them. White women need me to believe I can earn beauty, because when I want what I cannot have, what they have becomes all the more valuable.

I refuse them.

I also refuse the men. Oh, the men. I wish I could save this for another essay that I would promise to write but never do. Women's desire for beauty is a powerful weapon for exploitation. Even if the desire is natural, in that it is rational and also subconsciously coercive, open wanting against a backdrop of predatory constructs of cross-gender interactions is dangerous for women. There is an entire industry of men, self-proclaimed pickup artists, who sell their strategies for landing women. One of the most common techniques involves negging. This is when a man approaches a woman whose embodied beauty exceeds his own status. She is "out of his league." His league is typically determined by height, penis size, sexual experience, body type, and money, but also can take into account tastes and preferences. Some men say they turn to pickup artistry when the preferences so well suited to their social position—say, voting for a reviled political candidate or playing certain types of video games—

are devalued in mate markets. Once a woman is identified, the pickup artist might compliment her style, but mention that her teeth are imperfect. This is supposed to destabilize the woman, make her question what power she holds in the exchange, and eventually mold her into a more docile subject for sexual conquest.

Good men love to mock pickup artists and negging as evidence of their goodness. But good men also consume beauty, contributing much to its value. Without good men, the socio-cultural institution of Big Beauty could not be as powerful as it is. Big Beauty encompasses the norms that shape desirable traits in a romantic partner but also acceptable presentations of women in work, at play, and in public. It is the industrial complex of cosmetics, enhancements and services that promise individual women beauty. The idea that Big Beauty is evil but good men are nice is part of Big Beauty's systematic charm.

Big Beauty is just negging without the slimy actor. The constant destabilization of self is part and parcel of beauty's effectiveness as a social construct. When a woman must consume the tastes of her social position to keep it, but cannot control the tastes that define said position, she is suspended in a state of being negged. A good man need only then to come along and capitalize on the moment of negging, exploit the value of negged women, and consume the beauty that negs. It is really quite neat, if you think about it.

For black women who are engaging black men with the assumption that sexual engagement is within the realm of possibility, negging develops a new depth. I suspect this is true of all nonwhite male-female interactions shaped by sexual potential. They may be moderated by their proximity to whiteness—a fair-skinned Latina might have a different depth of this experience than a darker-skinned Afro-Latina—but the relations still hold: women who are not white must contend with beauty through the gaze of white men *and* nonwhite men.[15] This is perhaps the hardest of all these situations for me to describe. How do I distill something that is so diffuse across my life? That is what the relationship between my agency, the constraints of beauty, and the structure of race feels like—it has always been a part of the threads that are stitching me.

What these black men seemed to have wanted is the easiest way to suspend me between their wanting and my own.
They needed me to reflect the duality of beauty regimes that
exist in their corner of the social world. That's the corner
where heterosexual masculinity does to them similar things
that heterosexual femininity does to me but differently,
at variable rates and with distinct political consequences.
But unlike the space from which I emerge, these black men
can poke holes in the walls that for me are impenetrable.
They must travel through sexual ideologies about bulls and
bucks, losing some skin as they scrape through the walls
that beauty erects around social status. That is why it is so
important for me, a sister and a sista, to reflect back at them
the dominant beauty structure of white femininity *and* the
subordinate beauty structure of black womanhood.

Black women have to both aspire to the unattainable
paradox of white beauty and cultivate its counterparadox
*because both must exist for black masculinity to retain the
privilege of moving between two social spaces of potential
mates.* If I reinforce the white beauty norm, then I reproduce
it in a way that benefits white women. If black masculinity

can or may or does benefit from having the option of hitching its star to white beauty, then it needs black women to play our part. But where there is dominance, there is also subordination. Black people have a whole structure of class and income and wealth and tastes and preferences. It stands to reason that we also have a construct of beauty that shapes and stratifies good black women and bad black women, and so on. If black masculinity benefits from the option of hooking up with black women, then it has to value at least the performance of black beauty. Playing my part would look like espousing what a thick black stallion I am, while coveting the beautiful white woman I could never become. If I play my part, black masculinity benefits. White women needed me to neg myself and black men needed me to neg them at the expense of myself. Either way, I was losing and I knew it.

Repeatedly people have said to me in their own way, from within their own stratified statuses, that I need to believe I am beautiful or can become beautiful—not for my own benefit, but because it serves so many others. I reject the implicit bid for solidarity from every single white woman and I reject every overture from a man who wants to convince me that I am beautiful. I want nice people with nice-enough politics to look at me, reason for themselves that I am worthy, and feel convicted when the world does not agree. God willing they may one day extrapolate my specific case to the general rule, seeing the way oppression marginalizes others to their personal benefit.

I do not have any issues of self-worth—well, no more than anyone who used to be young and now is not. I am sensible. I know the streets in pregentrified communities where old men will still look twice and someone behind a counter might give me an extra piece of something for free. I know that cute and attractive are categories that exist, with their own attended privileges. But none of these things negates the structural apparatus that controls access to resources and ad hoc designates those with capital as beauty's gate-keepers. When beauty is white and I am dark, it means that I am more likely to be punished in school, to receive higher sentences for crimes, less likely to marry, and less likely to marry someone with equal or higher economic status.[16] Denying these empirical realities is its own kind of violence, even when our intentions are good.

They say that beauty is in the eye of the beholder and that ugly is as ugly does. Both are lies. Ugly is everything done to you in the name of beauty.

Knowing the difference is part of getting free.

Dying to Be Competent

Recording my debut album, "I don't work here."
Featuring the hit singles, "Yes, I do have a tick-
et. I'm the keynote speaker." and "Yes, I know
this is the line for First Class." Droppin straight
FIRE bars!

—@aryanwashere, tweet, January 29, 2018,
2:25 p.m.

. . . the most murderous states are also the most
racist.

—Michel Foucault[1]

I never dreamed about weddings or boyfriends or babies. The first dream for my imagined future self that I can recall starts with a sound. I was maybe five years old and I wanted to click-clack. The click-clack of high heels on a shiny, hard floor. I have a briefcase. I am walking purposefully, click-clack-click-clack. That is the entire dream.

At various times in my life I have interpreted that dream in different ways. It could be that I wanted the money someone with a briefcase and purpose would presumably earn. For a while I worried that it meant I did not have the heart required for committed love because my early, simple lessons of work were that it precludes anything soft. Now I have settled on competency. I dreamed of being competent.

I am writing this in a freezing house in Virginia during a bitterly cold winter, because my heat is off. I have three space heaters ordered in a pique from Amazon Prime and the oven door open. The oven door is country. The Amazon Prime is so middle class. All in all, it is very me. For perhaps the first season in my life I can afford heat *and* food *and* transportation *and* housing *and* the consumption of a good middle-class person. My heat is not off because I cannot pay, but because I forgot to pay. No matter that I can pack my overnight bag like a winning game of Tetris or that I keep receipts for tax season, competency will always be a ritual in wish fulfillment.

I am not the only one in love with the idea of competence. It is a neoliberal pipe dream that generates no end of services, apps, blogs, social media stars, thought leaders, and cultural programming, all promising that we can be competent. If you are working irregular shifts like an estimated 3.2 million people in the United States are, you cannot control your time. The instability of constant work without a constant employer can make it hard to plan your life. Thriving in liberal capitalism requires planning for eventualities that you cannot control. You have to plan for when you will be sick, when your children will go to daycare, when you will spend a week at the beach and how long you might live. Productivity tools promise you control where the political economy says you cannot have any. You cannot predict how well the State or your family will care for you when you are old, but you can schedule to the minute how much time you spend this week reallocating your retirement account.

My favorite of all of these tools is LinkedIn.[2] LinkedIn is the dumbest of all the dumb websites created during our new digital age. That is my expert opinion. LinkedIn is dumb. The interface is bad. The platform architecture cannot figure out how to facilitate networking *and* self-promotion *and* neoliberal branding *and* presentation of self, so it just does all of those things badly. It isn't dynamic. It isn't quite static. It is the worst of each. You know a website is bad when its founder proclaims that "people use the website wrong!" He thinks you should only "endorse" people you know, but everyone who uses LinkedIn accepts any request for a connection or an endorsement, because I have to believe deep down we know that it doesn't matter. Despite being dumb and poorly designed and having a founder who blames the users for the site's bad architecture, people are strangely defensive about LinkedIn. I made a joke about it on Twitter once and five years later people are still responding to that tweet, angry that I would even mildly disparage it. I made myself a promise that I would never again publicly make light of LinkedIn, once I realized why people were so defensive.

LinkedIn is an exemplar of the promises technology makes but that neoliberalism can never fulfill. By all accounts, all workers feel increasingly anxious about their job security, income mobility, and quality of life. Poor workers and middle-class workers and even highly paid elite workers in western economies are anxious because of the demands that our accelerated digital society makes of us. We know that we could be outsourced, downsized, and eased out of a job or a career or an entire industry at a moment's notice. Despite our shared anxiety not all of us believe in a collective response to what is fundamentally a collective problem. The only thing we mostly agree on is that we are individuals with the "freedom" to be anxious as we please. What pleases us is any technocratic fairytale of how we can network enough to offset unstable employment.

Who needs a promotion when you can add fifty endorsements to your LinkedIn or five new connections to your third-grade best friend's brother? All the busywork produced by the technological society perversely creates new ways for technology to make our anxiety a profitable extractive regime. It is a vicious cycle. Such is the foolishness of wanting to be competent in a political economy that can only sell you ways to *feel* competent, but does not offer sufficient ways to enact competency.

That is a problem for us all, to a certain degree. But for some of us being competent has always been an illusion. Now, it is the nature of global capital and inequality to make us structurally incompetent. For black women, racism, sexism, and classism have always made us structurally incompetent. To a black woman living global inequality and technological change, the competency trap is a cumulative multifold iron cage of network effects in oppressive regimes.

I have never felt more incompetent than when I was pregnant. Pregnancy is not just resistant to the dictates of capitalism, it is hell on competency. I was four months or so pregnant, extremely uncomfortable, and at work when I started bleeding. Bleeding is against company policy almost everywhere. When you are a black woman, having a body is already complicated for workplace politics. Having a bleeding, distended body is especially egregious. When I started bleeding, I waited until I filed my copy, by deadline, before walking to the front of the building, where I called my husband to pick me up.

An hour or so later, I was in the waiting room of my obstetrics office on the good side of town. I chose the office based on the crude cultural geography of choosing a good school or which TJ Maxx to go to: if it is on the white, wealthy side of town, it must be good. For many people I am sure that the medical practice was actually good. The happy, normal, thin white women in the waiting room every time I visited seemed pleased enough. The office staff was effective. The nurses' hands were always warm when they stuck one up your vagina. The doctors were energetic. All in all, it was all I knew to ask for.

Until I started bleeding. That day I sat in the waiting

room for thirty minutes, after calling ahead and reporting my condition when I arrived. After I had bled through the nice chair in the waiting room, I told my husband to ask them again if perhaps I could be moved to a more private area to wait. The nurse looked alarmed, about the chair, and eventually ushered me back. When the doctor arrived, he explained that I was probably just too fat and that spotting was normal and he sent me home. Later that night my ass started hurting, the right side. Just behind the butt muscle and off a bit to the side. I walked. I stretched. I took a hot bath. I called my mother, The Vivian. Finally, I called the nurse. She asked me if my back hurt. I said no, which was true. My back was fine. It was my butt that hurt. The nurse said it was probably constipation. I should try to go to the bathroom. I tried that for all the next day and part of another. By the end of three days, my butt still hurt and I had not slept more than fifteen minutes straight in almost seventy hours.

I went to the hospital. Again, they asked about my back, implied that I had eaten something "bad" for me and begrudgingly, finally decided to do an ultrasound. The image showed three babies, only I was pregnant with one. The other two were tumors, larger than the baby and definitely not something I had eaten. The doctor turned to me and said, "If you make it through the night without going into preterm labor, I'd be surprised." With that, he walked out and I was checked into the maternity ward. Eventually a night nurse mentioned that I had been in labor for three days. "You should have said something," she scolded me.

I asked for pain medication, but I would have to wait until it was bad enough to warrant what they kept calling "the narcotic." After a week of labor pains that no one ever diagnosed, because the pain was in my butt and not my back, I could not hold off labor anymore. I was wheeled into a delivery operating room, where I slipped in and out of consciousness. At one point I awoke and screamed, "motherfucker." The nurse told me to watch my language. I begged for an epidural. After three eternities an anesthesiologist arrived. He glared at me and said that if I wasn't quiet he would leave and I would not get any pain relief. Just as a contraction crested, the needle pierced my spine and I tried desperately to be still and quiet so he would not leave me there that way. Thirty seconds after the injection, I passed out before my head hit the pillow.

When I awoke I was pushing and then my daughter was here. Barely breathing and four days too early for the Catholic hospital to try any medical intervention, she died shortly after her first breath. The nurse wheeled me out of the operating room to take me back to recovery. I held my baby the whole way, because apparently that is what is done. After making plans for how we would handle her remains, the nurse turned to me and said, "Just so you know, there was nothing we could have done, because you did not tell us you were in labor."

Everything about the structure of trying to get medical care had filtered me through assumptions of my incompetence. There it was, what I had always been afraid of, what I must have known since I was a child I needed to prepare to defend myself against, and what it would take me years to accept was beyond my control. Like millions of women of color, especially black women, I was churned through a healthcare machine that neglected and ignored me until I was incompetent. Pain short-circuits rational thought. It can change all of your perceptions of reality. If you are in enough physical pain, your brain can see what isn't there. Pain, like pregnancy, is inconvenient for bureaucratic efficiency and has little use in a capitalist regime. When the medical profession systematically denies the existence of black women's pain, underdiagnoses our pain, refuses to alleviate or treat our pain, healthcare marks us as incompetent bureaucratic subjects. Then it serves us accordingly.

The assumption of black women's incompetence—we cannot know ourselves, express ourselves in a way that the context will render legible, or that prompts people with power to respond to us as agentic beings—supersedes even the most powerful status cultures in all of neoliberal capitalism: wealth and fame. In 2017 Serena Williams gave birth to her daughter. She celebrated with an interview, as is the ritual custom of celebrity cultures. In the interview, Serena describes how she had to bring to bear the full force of her authority as a global superstar to convince a nurse that she needed a treatment. The treatment likely saved Serena's life. Many black women are not so lucky.

In the wealthiest nation in the world, black women are

dying in childbirth at rates comparable to those in poorer, colonized nations. The World Health Organization estimates that black expectant and new mothers in the United States die at about the same rate as women in countries such as Mexico and Uzbekistan.[3] The high mortality rate of black women in the United States has been documented by the CDC, which says that black women are 243 percent more likely to die from pregnancy- or childbirth-related causes than are white women.[4]

These are not new data. They aren't hard-to-find, if hard-to-accept, data. Medical doctors surely know about these disparities, right? Why, then, would a global superstar have to intervene so directly in her own postnatal care, and what does that say about how poorer, average black women are treated when they give birth? There is surely something to be said about black women's structural oppression and cumulative disadvantage that conditions our physical responses to pregnancy. But there is also something to say about a healthcare system's assumptions regarding competency when it comes to the delivery of care that is killing black women.

The evidence in healthcare is some of the most dire, but examples of racialized, gendered competence abound because we rely on organizations to allocate the resources that govern our human rights. Healthcare is a lot like education, in that it is primarily delivered through bureaucracy. People in the bureaucracies make decisions, but many of the decisions are made for people by the rules attached to every role and every routine interaction. All of those rules are assumptions, derived from cultural beliefs about people, bodies, illness, and health.

To get the "healthcare" promised by the healthcare bureaucracy, it helps tremendously if the bureaucracy assumes that you are competent. When I called the nurse and said that I was bleeding and in pain, the nurse needed to hear that a competent person was on the phone in order to process my problem for the crisis that it was. Instead, something about me and the interaction did not read as competent. That is why I was left in a general waiting room when I arrived, rather than being rushed to a private room with the equipment necessary to treat a pregnancy crisis. When my butt hurt, the doctors and nurses did not read that as a competent interpretation of contractions and so no one addressed my labor pains for over three days. At every step of the process of having what I would learn later was a fairly typical pregnancy for a black woman in the United States, I was rendered an incompetent subject with exceptional needs that fell beyond the scope of reasonable healthcare.

"Black babies in the United States die at just over two times the rate of white babies in the first year of their life," says Arthur James, an OB-GYN at Wexner Medical Center at Ohio State University in Columbus.[5] When my daughter died, she and I became statistics.

What I remember most about the whole ordeal, groggy from trauma and pain and narcotics, is how nothing about who I was in any other context mattered to the assumptions of my incompetence. I was highly educated. I spoke in the way one might expect of someone with a lot of formal education. I had health insurance. I was married. All of my status characteristics screamed "competent," but nothing could shut down what my blackness screams when I walk into the room. I could use my status to serve others, but not myself.

Sociologists try to figure out how ideologies like race and gender and class are so *sticky*. How is it that we have laid bodies down in streets, challenged patriarchy in courts, bled for fair wages, and still inequalities persist? The easiest answer is that racism and sexism and class warfare are resilient and necessary for global capitalism. The easy answer is not wrong, but it does not always tell us the whys and what-fors of how a middle-class black woman getting care in the good part of town in the United States of America has the same health outcome as a black woman anywhere in the colonized world.

Of course, black women know why intuitively. Patricia Hill Collins once called on the idea of controlling images, those stereotypes that are so powerful they flatten all empirical status differences among a group of people to reduce them to the most docile, incompetent subjects in a social structure.[6] Those are the memes of the fat black woman, gesticulating with the text "I'm a strong black woman I don't need no man" that circulate throughout our digital media culture. Controlling images have fallen a bit out of favor in the feminist literature, sometimes thought to be a taken-for-granted relic of older theory. But that is only if we confine our analysis to popular culture, where negative stereotypes do seem pedestrian. When we broaden our field of analysis to the political economy of incompetence—who is and who is not structurally viable as an agentic being across the domains of social life—controlling images regain some of their explanatory power.

Controlling images were never just about the object of study—popular culture memes or characters from movies and television shows—but about the process of reproducing structural inequalities in our everyday lives. Social psychologists study how we acknowledge and reproduce status groups like "man," "woman," "black," "white," "Asian," "poor," "rich," "novice," and "expert" in routine interactions. These are statuses of people that we recognize as meaningful categories. When we interact with someone, a few things happen. We size up the person we are engaging with, scanning for any risks to our own social status. You don't want to be the person who mistakes the company president for the janitor, for example. We also scan others' perception of us. This is how all kinds of impromptu moments of cooperation make our day go smoothly. It's the guy who sees you struggling to get something on the bus and coordinates the four people around you to help you get on. Or it's the three women in a fast food line who all grab for a baby's bottle just before it hits the floor. We cooperate in micromoments and in longer settings like the waiting room of a doctor's office. And, when we are cooperating with strangers or near strangers, we are using all kinds of ideas about status to make the interaction work to our benefit.

Let's take a small detour to get something out of the way. The prevalent perception of black women as unruly bodies and incompetent caretakers overrules even the most dominant stereotype about us, namely that we are superhuman. The image of black women as physically strong without any emotions vulnerable enough to warrant consideration is one of the greatest cultural exports from the racist, sexist U.S. hierarchy. We are undisciplined yet steadfastly committed to the care of others. At one time we were good nannies until global anti-blackness made the world's immigrant brown women cheaper to import. Even as black women caregivers became less desirable as actual emotional labor-for-hire, we have remained firmly lodged in the cultural imagination as "superwomen." It might seem that the culture's perennial strong woman would also be *competent*. But incompetent and superhero do not actually conflict in the context of essential notions about gender, race, class, and hierarchy.

Black women are superheroes when we conform to others' expectations of us. When we are sassy but not smart; successful but not happy; competitive but not actualized—then, we have some inherent wisdom. That wisdom's value is only validated by our culture when it serves someone or something else. We must inspire or provide the emotional release of "calling out" someone afflicted by the guilt of their unearned privilege. When we perform some existential service to men, to capital, to political power, to white women, and even to other "people of color" who are marginally closer to white than they are to black, then we are superwomen.[7] We are fulfilling our purpose in the natural order of things. When, instead, black women are strong in service of themselves, that same strength, wisdom, and wit become evidence of our incompetence.

The structural incompetence of black women is how

we were made into property makers without any rights to property during slavery; into Patrick Moynihan's ghosts of black family deviance in the 1960s; and today into icons whose embodiment of authentic emotion is transmuted into digital memes meant to show you're woke in the 2000s. As objectified superhumans, we are valuable. As humans, we are incompetent.

Back to how status works. The big categories that work in almost any context are diffuse status characteristics. Our beliefs about those categories are so rich, deep, historical, omnipresent, and shared by others whose esteem we value that they show up in almost any social interaction. Those are the categories on which organizations like schools and hospitals base their bureaucratic assumptions. Who is a doctor? Man, white, maybe Asian (East not South and god knows rarely Southeast). Who is a nursing assistant? Woman, brown, black. Of course, values come with those assumptions. Doctors are good. Man, white, maybe Asian (East not South and god knows rarely Southeast) is also good. And so forth and so on. The great promise of social progress is that we can each earn other status descriptors like "expert" or "medical professional." You go to school. You deny yourself a little fun here and there. You sacrifice. You conform. And people out there recognizing your specific status characteristics is supposed to be the reward. In interactions someone might assume a woman cannot do math, but learn that she is an engineer. The question is, which status characteristic will win out?

More often than not the hierarchy of diffuse status characteristics overpowers any status characteristics that we earn. Patricia Hill Collins's matrix of domination, the intersecting planes of privilege and domination, still matters.[8] If we read that oeuvre more deeply, attuned to the ways that capital and neoliberalism have inculcated greater incompetence for more and more people, we find that what black feminists promised all along was true: to know the most present marginalized oppressions is to know the future.

Being structurally incompetent injects friction into every interaction, between people, and between people and organizations, and between organizations and ideologies. Frictionless living is the promise of neoliberal capital—that is, if you are on the winning side of power. But when black women in the United States are dying trying to give birth and their babies are dying trying to get born, not simply because of poverty but because the grotesque accumulation of capital in the West is predicated on our structural incompetence, then we can see the ends of hypercapitalism in daily life.

This moment of global inequality demands incompetent subjects. The status quo and ever-intensifying versions of it require incompetent consumers who will learn to want technological solutions to their political problems. Are you starving even though there is food? Here is an app to connect you with the charity that is filling that hole in our ragged social safety net. Are global profits being extracted by the financial class while driving down wages and quality of work, even for people with expensive college educations? Here is a website where you can purchase a credential that might help you get a new job, one where you will likely be in the same position again in eighteen months. Your structural incompetence generates ever more sophisticated consumption goods, goods that reinforce status games of who is deserving and who is not.

Did you use the app to get a job or to become an entrepreneur? Do you use social media like a customer or a producer? Are you surveilled by the state like poor people or do you surveil yourself like the middle class? These gradations of difference are meaningless if the question is which consumption status group has power over their political incompetence. All of them are incompetent; they only differ in how they can afford to lie to themselves about it.

What so many black women know is what I learned as I sat at the end of a hallway with a dead baby in my arms. The networks of capital, be they polities or organizations, work most efficiently when your lowest status characteristic is assumed. And once these gears are in motion, you can never be competent enough to save your own life.

That is how black feminism knows the future.

Know Your Whites

The origins of property rights in the United States are rooted in racial domination. Even in the early years of the country, it was not the concept of race alone that operated to oppress Blacks and Indians; rather, it was the interaction between conceptions of race and property that played a critical role in establishing and maintaining racial and economic subordination.

—Cheryl I. Harris, *Whiteness as Property*[1]

Barack Obama's election was a catalyst for a level of voter suppression activities that had not been seen so clearly or disturbingly in decades.

—Carol A. Anderson, *White Rage*[2]

A year before it was real, the very idea of a President Barack Obama was ridiculous to me. I was and am southern, god bless. I am black. I come from black people who are southerners even when they were New Yorkers for a spell. We are the black American story of enslavement, rural migration, urban displacement, resistance, bootstrapping, mobility, and class fragility. In this milieu we, as a friend once described it, know our whites. To know our whites is to understand the psychology of white people and the elasticity of whiteness. It is to be intimate with some white persons but to critically withhold faith in white people categorically. It is to anticipate white people's emotions and fears and grievances, because their issues are singularly our problem. To know our whites is to survive without letting bitterness rot your soul.

That is what I was working with when I went to my first Obama house party in 2007—a few generations' worth of lived and inherited expertise in knowing our whites. Our whites are southern, like me. Even if they spent some time in places north and west, to become white in the South is to absorb some large part of its particular iteration of the U.S. racial hierarchy. The house party was being held in Myers Park, a lush, wealthy in-town enclave in Charlotte, North Carolina. Charlotte was my home. I knew Myers Park as a place and a cultural geography of the city's racist histories. Myers Park is gorgeous. The streets are wide. The homes are stately without being garish. The residents are mere miles from the center of the city's banking, employment, transportation, and entertainment hubs. As neighborhoods throughout Charlotte fell victim to blight during the housing crash of the 2000s, Myers Park remained stable, thriving even, with housing values continuing upward trends year over year.[3]

Myers Park is also, as one with even a cursory knowledge of how wealth works in the United States would know, the beneficiary of years of racist covenant restrictions and redlining. Myers Park is beautiful because it has encoded its whiteness into the mundane market transactions that we rarely see: zoning, planning, investment, homeowners associations. White people in Myers Park, no matter where they are from at any time in their lives, are *of* Myers Park whether they acknowledge it or not.

I grew up knowing those whites. They mostly go to private school. When they don't, they make the public high school (Myers Park High School, naturally) function like a private school.[4] We call this opportunity hoarding, and it looks something like this: white parents use their economic privilege to purchase homes in communities that have benefited from generations of wealth privilege. That wealth privilege generates investment in streets, sidewalks, greenspace, traffic lights, clean air, proper waste treatment, and safe drinking water. When white families purchase in these neighborhoods they are also purchasing access to the local public school. That is because we assign students in the U.S. public school system, for the most part, by their home zip codes. Once enrolled in these schools by virtue of having the income to live in communities that are built on the stabilizing forces of generational wealth, these families generally prize "diversity."

They are good people. They want all the children in their child's school to thrive, but they want their child to thrive just a bit more than most. To help their child thrive, these parents use their proximity to local and civic leaders to lobby their personal preferences as politically expedient positions. They gently but insistently marshal resources like teacher time, curriculum access, and extracurricular participation for their children. They donate. They volunteer. They call. They email. They make this already well-funded public school work like a private school for their child: individualized attention, personalized resources, and cumulative advantage. The opportunities these parents hoard become zero-sum for parents who cannot do the same. The families that can hoard do, and the neighborhoods in which they live benefit.

For a spell, Myers Park was at the heart of the nation's public relations tour for post–Civil Rights era integration.

The wealthy white families of the community had mostly supported busing their students into the historically black West Charlotte High School. They believed in diversity. Once there, a rising tide of investment in the resource-starved black high school seemed to benefit all . . . but the white students benefited most. The experiment in integration lasted but thirty years.

Myers Park is typical of a national pattern of how segregated lives and intertwined cross-racial fortunes play out. But, Myers Park performs resegregation differently than some other urban-suburban enclaves, if only for how very *southern* its residents are in articulating their privilege. The homes are large but not plantation-like. They are the kinds of old homes that toothy gentrifiers on HGTV remodeling shows say have "good bones." I am almost certain "good bones" means "worth however much money this pit is about to suck from you because the neighborhood is reliably white," but I digress. Myers Park is neighborly, even to strangers, before dark. It has manners. There are porches, even if few people sit on them, preferring, instead, the safety of the backyard. Social networks are cultivated at the local church—it is the South, after all—and cemented through business partnerships. Myers Park people donate, their money and their time, to good causes. And these perfectly civil people live in intentionally cultivated, nominally diverse, in-town panopticons that need no guard in the central watchtower but whiteness.

Charlotte, North Carolina, is full of middle-class blacks, activist black people of all classes, organized third- and fourth-generation Latinos. I could not believe the Obama house party was happening in Myers Park, of all places in the city. Today I cannot imagine it anywhere else.

The party was in one of the homes usually only accessible to someone like me when, twice a year, you can pay $15 or so for one of those charity parades of homes. I was early. When I rang the bell a young white woman, still wet from a shower, told me to come on in, but no one was yet there. I sat for almost half an hour as they finished preparing, acutely aware of my social faux pas. As people arrived, of all ages and walks of life, I was the only black person until almost an hour into the house party. That is when a brother carrying a bicycle arrived with his white girlfriend.

The hosts asked for donations without stuttering the way that I still do when I have to do "the ask." It was taken for granted that you had come to spend money and had money to spend. Here, a full eight years before mobile credit card payments would penetrate my black hair salon or Saturday swap meets, the hosts took mobile payments using a website. The whites in this room were all in for Obama. They talked about him like old black people talk about Martin Luther King. They loved his biography. They embraced his political mantra. They were positive he could win.

Back at home, the black people I know were positive that white people were crazy to think that he could win. My mother told me as much: "White people are crazy," The Vivian said. She, like me, knew her whites. I went home that night of the house party and told her that I had seen, not new whites, but white people doing what people do: coalescing around shared interests. Only, their interests converged with my own. They still had more money, more power than we had. They were as young as me, but lived in million-dollar estates. They would still negotiate the daily experience of racial segregation in their neighborhoods and schools and jobs, but they had, for countless reasons, chosen this black man as "their guy." The question I could not parse for many years was why.

There is no need to rehash our national identity crisis at the election of the first African American (if not black American) U.S. president. Fox News scaled new heights of shrill paranoia. Then they built a stair lift to the top for their predominantly white, elderly audience. African Americans did not believe the election had happened until a month before the end of Obama's second, and final, term. Many black Americans, of all national origins but with shared political ideologies, struggled to find a way to critique the imperialist office without disparaging the man occupying it. Hispanic voters and Asian American voters were divided in their support by national origin, generational status, and income.[5] But in almost every ethnic community there was a strong contingent seeking their own people's story in Obama's.

The times were not idyllic, but they were as close to multicultural as the U.S. public sphere has ever felt. Those are the eight years that writer Ta-Nehisi Coates calls the "Good Negro Government period."[6] Like the eight years of Black Reconstruction some 130 years prior to his first presidential contest—one that he would win handily—Obama's Good Negro Government period was marked by black political competence and white fear. Political analyst Jamelle Bouie once said, during a joint interview we recorded for a radio program, that in the twilight of Obama's final term it occurred to him that if this safely competent black man was not good enough for white America, then he would never be.[7] It was heart-wrenching listening to Jamelle discover this fundamental truth of being black in America. And it was for me indeed a fundamental truth.

How could I explain the hope of that Myers Park house party *and* my core truth that whiteness necessitates black subjugation? This paradox—that is what it is, because these truths seem to occupy opposing sides but in reality are the same side of a Janus-faced coin—mirrored the national paradox: how could the same nation that elected Barack Obama immediately elect Donald Trump? The answer was not in Obama's blackness. Blackness is not a paradox.

Blackness *is*. It has to be for whiteness, at any point in time or space, to enact its ultimate expression: elasticity.

Whiteness, the idea, the identity tethered to no nation of origin, no place, no gods, exists only if it can expand enough to defend its position over every group that challenges the throne. White is being European until it needs to also be Irish because of the Polish who can eventually be white if it means that Koreans cannot. For that situational dominance to reproduce itself, there must be a steady pole. That pole is blackness. And so the paradox of how we could elect Obama and Trump is not in how black Obama is or is not. It is, instead, in how white he is (or, is not). The Obama-Trump dialectic is not progress-backlash but do-si-do; one dance, the same steps, mirroring each other, and each existing only in tandem.

Like whiteness itself, Obama was because Trump is.

White voters allowed Barack Obama to become an idea and a president because he was a fundamental projection of the paradox that defines them as white. I almost forgot once. Old trees and new whites are a seduction. But my soul remembers my grandmother's memories. It is imperative that one knows one's whites.

"I've never seen anything like it, Ma," I told her. "But this black man can win."

Today, my mother has no fewer than nineteen portraits and commemorative magazine covers of Barack and Michelle Obama on her mantelpiece. She has exactly four pictures of me, for reference. She has only one of her husband, something that annoys him to no end. She hung up the phone with me any time Barack was giving a speech and she would, I am sure, trade me for Sasha and Malia in a heartbeat. But back in 2007, The Vivian could not believe that a black man with a funny name who so clearly did not know his whites stood a chance. She was finally convinced to believe that whites were different, had perhaps evolved like the far end of the paint store: ecru, pearl, eider, snow, star, toque. It was another Myers Park house party that did the trick. I dragged her there. She almost did not get out of the car. But when she did, she saw it too. It wasn't Barack

Obama knowing his whites that convinced me or my mother. It was that whites knew Obama.

In the forensic account of his final days as president, writers opined about Obama's faith in white America as fundamentally good, humane, and, above all, capable of evolution. It is easy to believe that this mattered. We all like seeing ourselves through the eyes of those who hold us in esteem, perhaps especially so when we know that we have failed to earn it. We want to be redeemable. And a nation's father figure is a good person to have believe in you. It is especially good when you suspect, on some level, that the father figure might have a good reason to doubt you.

The eternally future-looking American story is about a tomorrow that is disconnected from yesterday precisely because the story of the nation does not come off particularly well in that retelling. But I have come to believe that it did not matter that Obama had faith in white people. They needed only to have faith in him: in his willingness to reflect their ideal selves back at them, to change the world without changing them, to change blackness for them without being black to them.

Obama's "hybridity" and "two-ness" and "biracial" identity may have mattered. It did not matter because of how it
shaped Obama, but because of how it made white voters
feel about themselves. In sociology, there are several theories
about those who are born or socialized into two cultures
at once. These people have been called liminal or margin-
al, for being suspended between two societies. The black
world and white world that Ta-Nehisi described in his grand
essay on Obama's presidency "My President Was Black," are
often tossed about casually. It is important to understand
them more precisely.[8]

There is a black norm only because there is a white norm,
and vice versa. Some would argue that people like Obama
exist in both spaces simultaneously and thus someone like
Obama has special insight into both cultures. That insight
supposedly breeds empathy. That kind of empathy may be
why Obama could look at years of pictures of his wife and
children drawn as apes and decades of white suppression
of perceived black socioeconomic gains as racial, albeit not
racist: "I'm careful not to attribute any particular resistance
or slight or opposition to race."[9] That is catnip to millions
of white voters.

The other interpretation of liminality, or double-consciousness, that Obama is said to represent is more complicated. Not only does one trapped between two sets of social norms understand each better, but he is often blinded to the ways in which they are in conflict. Duality can breed insight, but it can also breed delusion. Holding two sets of social selves, two ways of being and understanding the world at one time, may soften the edges so much that for the liminal, the edges no longer exist.

Obama, in his own writings and in the voluminous writings about him, seems to think that he could only ever really "embraced" or "chosen" blackness. He seems to truly believe that he exercised some great act of charity and agency in adopting black cool. My first black president seems to think that he could raise his daughters to believe in systemic racism without legitimizing the idea of systemic reparations. He thinks that he can be his brother's keeper without changing the policies, laws, and investments that keep his brothers in bad jobs, in poor neighborhoods, with bad educational options, and at the bottom of the social hierarchy. My first black president seems to think he can have black cool without black burden. For all his intimacies with his white mother and white grandparents, my first black president doesn't appear to know his whites.

There's no other way to explain Obama's inability to imagine that this nation could elect Donald Trump. Those of us who know our whites know one thing above all else: whiteness defends itself. Against change, against progress, against hope, against black dignity, against black lives, against reason, against truth, against facts, against native claims, against its own laws and customs. Even after Donald Trump was elected, Obama told Coates that all is not lost. He is still hopeful about the soul of white America. He said nothing about the soul of black America. That is where my hope resides.

While many things change, my hope in the soul of black America remains constant. It is not an uncritical faith, but it is an invaluable heuristic for days such as ours. For instance, I was never confused about why this nation would elect Donald Trump. I was never deeply hurt when it did so. I cry and am angered by and passionate about what Trump's election is doing to human beings and social institutions. But I am not disappointed. If you truly know your whites, disappointment rarely darkens your door. That is because knowing your whites is to know that white voters allowed Barack Obama to become an idea and a president because he was a charming projection of the paradox that defines them as white. The charm is neither necessary nor sufficient, but it helps.

What *is* necessary for the paradox of whiteness to maintain the internal tension that defines it is for superiority to coexist with fragility.[10] As the nation that bears most fully the stamp of whiteness's authentic expression, the United States is full of such paradoxes: slaveholders building a republic from the embers of the Enlightenment; freedom of speech that must delineate acceptable speech if any speech is to be free; equal opportunity that necessitates inequality of outcomes.

These paradoxes were in full flower at a 2015 Trump rally. I decided to attend that rally because, really, how could I be surprised by any of it? I was living in the capital of Virginia, the former home of the Confederacy, in a building rumored to sit atop a mass grave for the enslaved, and no one seemed to believe Donald Trump could win. The narrative went: no nation that had progressed enough to elect Obama could turn around and elect the pleathery, oft orange-tinged reality TV show host who sometimes played a billionaire on shock radio. I talked to sensible people, smart people, deeply knowledgeable people. I talked to working-class people and middle-class people and whatever the people are who go to boarding schools. I talked to journalists and political organizers and fundraisers and activists and students and professors. Only two people in my daily sphere believed it was not only possible, but probable: Ms. Yvette and the Guy I Talk to Behind the Building on His Smoke Break (Guy, for short).

Ms. Yvette used to clean our office. Roughly 3 percent of the nation's 1.6 million full-time faculty members are black. I am one of them. I can be the only one all day every day. Seeing Ms. Yvette is frequently my only chance to speak in my mother tongue when I am not home. It did not take much to get Ms. Yvette talking. It did not take much to get almost any black person at the time to talk about the election.

"Girl you see what's his name?"

"Oh yeah, I saw it. Child, child, child. It's a mess."

"It is but it ain't our mess!"

"Well, I hope it isn't anyway."

"You think he gonna win?"

We looked at each other and started laughing. Of course he would win. The idea that he could not was ridiculous. Ms. Yvette knew her whites.

Guy may work where I work. He may not. It isn't very clear. Something about our routine daily activities is aligned. We pass each other at least twice a week during a semester. Sometimes he is wearing a uniform. He is almost always smoking. Sometimes it is even just a tobacco cigarette.

Guy is serious about calling me Professor.

"Professor Ma'am, you see your boy on TV?"

"How is he my boy?"

"He ain't mine!"

"Mine either."

"You think he gonna win?"

"Man, look. I believe anything is possible."

"Yeah, you seen Katt Williams? That one about the tiger? That tiger bit your ass because he remembered he was a tiger."[11]

Guy got it.

———

I would not have dreamed of going to the Trump rally alone. I also would not have dreamed of asking Ms. Yvette or Guy. I had to go with white people. There were two of them and one of me. We had strategy sessions beforehand. I would walk between them, minimizing chances for small talk with the Trump faithful. We would sit near an exit, again with me between them, close to the end of the row. My comfort level would dictate when we left, no questions asked.

I was not there to see Donald Trump. He was a known quantity. I was there to see the people who believed in Donald Trump as the leader of the free world. I scanned the parking lot at the convention center. I noticed how many nice cars there were. Big trucks, expensive trucks, but also luxury sedans and sports cars. I inventoried the bumper stickers: University of Virginia, George Mason University, Old Dominion University, churches, resort towns, and peeling mainstream party stickers from elections past.

You could not just enter the convention center. Virginia had seen its share of recent public disturbances. A good tenth of a mile before the entrance, you had to verbally declare to a uniformed guard whether you were there to attend the rally or to protest it. The two groups were separated, sent behind opposing barricades. I stood behind a group of four white women, late forties and early fifties. It was hot. They wore the short-shorts and visors of vacationers. They were also drunk like vacationers. One proclaimed loudly, as one would at a rock concert, that if she caught Donald Trump's eye she was going to flash her "tits" because "gawd, he is so sexy."

The audience inside was bored. These rallies are not electrifying. By the time you see them as slick media packages on TV or the internet, editing makes it look like a party. It is far more mundane than that. Babies wore onesies that said, "Lock the bitch [Hillary Clinton] up." Mothers bought drink koozies with crass sayings about "balls" and "hags" on them for their accompanying teenage sons. From the swag to the speakers, the Trump rally rhetoric was violent. But the mood and the scene was almost as placid as that Myers Park street. People smiled and nodded at me, if a little confused about seeing me. They had manners. One man in a wheelchair hooted, "Crooked bitch" when the topic of the American Health Care Act was mentioned from the dais.

Later, he mimed moving his manual wheelchair a bit so that I could move by him easily. Asian American immigrants, mostly first and second generation according to their signs, cheered when Trump disparaged immigrants. A handful of black (maybe African American, but I cannot be certain) people throughout the crowd sat back throughout the rally, tapping feet or patting knees at the parts they liked.

Much has been made of the losers who voted for Trump. I do not mean that disparagingly, but descriptively, as the Trump voter is generally typed as one who has lost something: economic opportunities, financial security, identity, gender supremacy. Not all losers do so gracefully. People ate up the idea of Trump voters as losers. It is empathetic and, perhaps more importantly given how white and elite is the media profession, confirmation bias. Others pointed out, rightfully so, that the Trump coalition is not a historical anomaly. Viewed through the lens of historical struggle, Trump's election could be seen as white voters reclaiming this nation as theirs. All useful ways to understand a multifaceted phenomenon. One lens struggles to explain the empirical data showing that the typical Trump voter was, in fact, middle class and educated.

The other is more helpful if we consider that historical progress and reclamations exist as one equation. But there is still
something missing.

Political theorist Corey Robin understands the history of
the conservative right in the United States as a search for a
fight, because the act of being conservative necessitates an
undesirable progress against which it can rebel. In a sort
of manifestation politics, the "right" co-creates or at least
abets social progress against which it can be juxtaposed.
Staid conservatism is far from seeking stasis. It is provoking
and reactive because without progress there is no reason to
prefer the lack of progress. Similarly, what is a white republic for white citizens and in defense of white property if there
is not a dark threat? To the extent that white racial identity
matters at all to how white voters vote, white Obama voters
and white Trump voters are not necessarily expressing different views of whiteness. They are expressing the same one,
each necessary for the other and both required for white
identity politics to exist at all.

In its fragility—ceding ground to Obama's multicultural
vision of a majority-minority America—whiteness expresses

its superiority. The people at the Trump rally were not losers, neither were they especially remarkable. For all its violent rhetoric, the rally was quaint. The sameness of Myers Park's lawns and rules about arriving early exerted whiteness as surely as a multicultural, mixed-class audience at the Trump rally projected their faith in whiteness as this nation's most redeeming attribute. I however am not sure what social progress would actually look like given that its existence relies on the paradox of whiteness. But I do believe like Guy: a tiger bites to remind you that it is a tiger.

Black Is Over
(Or, Special Black)

I'm looking for a mixed girl

Asian, Jamaican

I'm looking for a mixed girl

Puerto Rican, Haitian

I'm looking for a mixed girl

Cuban and White

I'm trying to get mixed up tonight like

Excuse me miss, what's your name, where ya
from, can I come

—T-Pain, "Mix'd Girl"

"**B**lack people are over." That is how it was said to me once. The occasion was a meeting of professors who were working together on a student project. It was a "people of color" cabal. If pressed to do so at a glance, one might have said that everyone in the room was black. In a discussion of methods and theories and other such things that comprise a significant part of my job, one of the women—we were all women—said assuredly that we have moved on, past black and white. Hence, "black people are over." I did not feel over and I am most certainly black. But it was said so casually because of the kind of black that I am presumed to be in rooms such as these. There have been many such rooms and I end up in more of them, more frequently, the more I inch up the class ladder. The proclamation makes a mistake of assuming that black people, like me, were only ever a problem and not a people.

But, first, just what kind of black am I? It is actually a common question. A senior scholar of great standing in my profession once said to me, "I do not trust you. Too many white people like you." Which, ouch. He also told me that being a dark black woman would prove a problem for me in academia. I am glad a man finally told me that, I tell you what. This was all said with great affection, by the way. I had passed a test for what kind of black I was. It is a political question—do I align myself with the interests of black people? I do. Only, the question can be more complicated depending on which black people are in question.

Do I align myself with black people across the diaspora? With black people on the political left or the political right? With black people who have a nonblack parent? With black people who prefer *African American* or *nigga*? The easy answer is that I am basic black. The harder answer is that it's never as easy as it sounds. What has been offered to me or denied me in parts, at different times, are opportunities to agree that black people are over. I can never know what the people who offer me this are thinking, but it seems that the offer is conditioned on that darkness and womanness the great man scholar told me would be a professional problem.

This was not a problem I remember experiencing growing up. I knew that not all black people were like us. I spent time in New York with Dominicans and black Puerto Ricans who would fight if you called them black. One of my mother's best friends was a Haitian chef named Henry George. He did wonderful, unholy things to fish. We traveled. I knew black people came from all over the world.

Once, I liked a Dominican boy named Nigel. We were play-hide-and-go-get-it-years-old. I was dark, as has been established. It had never been an issue for me before. Despite a world's obsession with colorism, where the darker people of almost every nationality are marginalized relative to their lighter and whiter kin, I grew up in a bubble. Nigel tried to get me. I did not try very hard not to let him. In 1980s preteen culture that made us the neighborhood Brangelina for the summer. It was a simpler time.

It was simple until Nigel's older brother caught us kissing behind the house. He was not upset about the kissing part. He was more than upset about the black American part. He told Nigel not to let their family catch him. He meant with me. Do not let his family catch him with me. I was so precious that I did not understand the admonishment until much later when my worldlier cousin explained that Dominicans do not date black-black girls. Not dark black, although that was certainly part of it. But black-black. Regular black. The kind of black that we are is over.

In sociology, we often refer to black people who are in the United States but who are not descendants of either the enslaved or, later, of those who experienced the Great Migration as "black ethnics." It is a complicated term because it implies that black Americans do not have an ethnicity.[1] In layman's terms we are usually trying to differentiate black people who are born in the United States from those who were not. There is some intuitive understanding that black ethnics have a distinct culture but that they are also captured in the anti-blackness dragnet that does not ask if you have an accent before it shoots you.

As I have argued elsewhere in this volume, whiteness has the political power to be elastic. Originating as it does not from nation or kin but from the primordial ooze of capitalism, whiteness can only be defined by state power. It requires a legal system that can formalize irrational biological expressions, making them rational. It needs a justice system that will adjudicate the arbitrary inclusion and exclusion of people across time. And, most of all, whiteness requires a police state that can use violent force to defend its sovereignty. Blackness is necessarily static as a counterweight to whiteness. Black ethnics have always complicated whiteness's desire for cheap labor and ideological mascots because what is real and perceived about them challenges blackness as a fixed, homogenous biological project that supersedes culture, nation, and environment. The reality of that imagined blackness has never held.

How you experience the heterogeneity of blackness depends in large part on where you grow up. In the U.S. South, close as we were to interstate highways that truck cargo from Canada to Mexico and back, we were more likely to have

Mexicans around us than we were to know Dominicans. In New York, black is as fluid as the heat waves that rise from the sidewalks in August. You can walk through five Littles in five blocks: Little Haiti, Little Jamaica, Little Nigeria, Little Trinidad, Little Ethiopia. Out west in California, Afro-Latino culture and black American culture are historically intertwined. Growing up in the South, my experience with black ethnics as a steady presence was limited to summers and vacations. That was true through college. Graduate school was something else.

For the first time in my educational career, I was attending a predominantly white school. And, also for the first time, I had reason to become intimately juxtaposed against different class hierarchies that pried apart my racial identity from my class identity. I had attended majority-minority schools for most of my primary schooling. My high school was historically and majority black during my tenure. And I had chosen to attend a historically black college for undergrad. This had never felt strange to me until my first days at Emory University.

Emory University is white. I mean, literally white. Almost

the entire campus is constructed from white Georgian marble. You could outfit a lifetime's worth of HGTV kitchens with the rubble of Emory's architecture. I remember walking along, my first day on campus, and thinking that this must be what it is like to be trapped alive in a mausoleum. A mausoleum of whiteness. So very white.

My cohort was also so very white. It was full of lovely people, but, save for three of the maybe thirty students I regularly engaged with on campus, they were all white. But the university knows all of the right things to do about "diversity," a bullshit term invented by bureaucrats who stutter when they say "black." In the modern university, a good liberal arts school believes in equal opportunity. It welcomes diversity.[2] It promotes that diversity in all of its marketing materials. Some go so far as to have more nonwhite students in their marketing than they do in their classes.[3] Such a university defines diversity broadly. It includes international students and differently abled students and sexual minorities and so forth and so on. It would likely include height if it could. What matters here is that diversity is good and to demonstrate its commitment to diversity the university sponsors a black graduate student association. In search of survival, I signed up for the very first meeting of the Black Graduate Student Association.

The meeting was about the important things: where to get our hair done, what clubs were popping, and what side of town everyone lived on so that we could socialize. Then, the conversation turned to area soca clubs and Brazilian salons. I love soca. I love a Brazilian blowout. I was with it. And then someone in the room asked, "Where do the local black-black people go?" so that it could be avoided. I was taken aback. I identified with those local black-black people. In fact, the high density of local black-black people was a big part of why I had chosen a school located in Atlanta, Georgia. The comment went unremarked upon, taken for granted as a reasonable concern for this group. That is when I looked more closely at the room.

The black graduate student association at Emory University was black, broadly defined. And, given the university's preference for students who could be both black *and* some other kind of diversity category, many of those students were black ethnics: Nigerian, Beninese, Jamaican, Cape Verdean,

Dominican, Haitian.[4] It is a sticky thicket to discuss, but for many reasons, black ethnic students and faculty can bring cachet to a university that plain black students, like me, cannot. Nothing about the logistics of this makes sense materially. One academic administrator once said of a California school that faculty and administration were more enthused about diversifying their faculties through international black ethnics than U.S. black professors, despite the former having more upfront hiring costs.

At elite universities especially, administrators and faculty view black ethnic students as better prepared than U.S. black students. As a Duke University professor once put it to me, "African students appreciate their educations," which I took to mean black ethnic students presumably cause fewer problems than regular blacks. From the students' perspectives, U.S. universities are a part of a postcolonial game of western credentialism where those with the means in nations beset by extreme income inequality purchase a pathway into the global labor market. Just as is true of international students from China, Japan, and India who find their way to the United States, our universities are generally cherry-picking the winners of extreme social stratification in other countries through our admissions processes. The black ethnic students in that room were no more representative of their home nations than I am of the United States. But in an oppressively white school we are all "black" in a way that should matter and that should flatten these differences, with various degrees of success.

That is because class matters, and so does culture. Those are deeply intertwined, class and culture. Graduate school moved me up a rung or two in social class mobility. There is not much money attached to doctoral studies, but social class is about more than money. It is about attitudes and culture and tastes. And Emory certainly had attitudes, culture, and tastes that were different from those in my previous educational institutions. By moving up I had also moved into a space where blackness was more contested than I had ever before experienced. This is the moment when I was supposed to learn that black is over.

Black was so over that it was not even a serious field of study in my academic department. The department at the time was so wholly uninterested in black people and the study of black life that for several years the graduate students taught all the undergraduate courses in race. In such spaces, you have to build buffers for your emotional and mental health. That is how I ended up at dinner one night with about seven or eight black people in academia. Most of us were graduate students. We were there to kiss the ring of a visiting professor and to talk to other black people for a little while. The visiting professor introduced me around with great fanfare. I was brilliant, a phenom, really going places. He had to say that because he had once been my professor. He was responsible for me. This kind of thing is also the way the people at the table are supposed to know how to treat you, a very big deal in an insular work world like mine.

Because I was such a big deal to an actual big deal, the black man seated to my left made a great effort at small talk. I wish he had not bothered. I hate small talk. It is small. Small is for teacups and occasionally for tiny houses. Too much small talk is how a country is given to sociopaths who thrive on shallow chatter to distract their emotional sleight of hand. Talk should be meaningful or kept to a minimum.

We moved quickly through the basics. What do we study? How is school going? Teaching or research? Finally, the man moved on to who I was rather than what I was: "So, where are you from?" An easy question. I am from North Carolina. "No, I mean where are you *from*?" I am not confused, but perhaps he is, so I say it again. I am from North Carolina. He got a little frustrated, as if I were being deliberately obtuse.

Here is where anyone who does not look white or black will find me ridiculous. Such people are asked all the time where they are from. People ask the question of persons whose physical or cultural presentation disrupts the questioner's intuitive understanding of race. Black people do not have blue eyes—where are you from? Asians are from China and Japan, but you are brown—where are you from? You are blond but you are speaking Spanish, which is what Mexicans speak—where are you from?

The question is not strange for its being asked, but for its being asked of me. My entire life I have had absolutely no gap between how I perceive myself and how the world perceives me. I identify as exactly what I look like I am. It is a kind of

privilege in a world where conforming to somatic expectations of race, gender, and sexuality minimizes invasions of
your privacy and property. But it is a complicated privilege.

The privilege got very complicated that night. Overhear-
ing the conversation, the visiting professor intervened with
a laugh. "He means what kind of special negro are you?" I
eventually unpacked it all. I was in a room where I was presented as exceptional. And, in this man's mind, exceptional
black people are not regular domestic black people, especially in a profession that promotes the idea of black ethnics
as superior black people. These are the black people who
are less likely to agitate for a course on race in a sociology
program too unbothered to be embarrassed that they do not
have one. These are the black people who bring status to the
student body by being international. You can offer Jamaican food in the cafeteria during the diversity menu week
without being racist. Were I as exceptional as I had been
introduced to be, in this room full of people who were filtered through that institutional process, it would have been
reasonable to assume that I was a kind of black who would
have a better answer than "North Carolina" to "Where are

you from?" That is, it was reasonable to assume that I was not black-black.

Over the years I have had strangers try repeatedly to make me over into a different kind of black. There was the Nigerian tennis player I dated for a while. He liked very much to introduce me as "the woman getting her Ph.D." Didn't I have any African in my family? I certainly looked like it, he suggested. And, if I did, it would make introducing me all the better. There was the man in Massachusetts who refused to accept that I was not West African. The basis for his incredulity was the Harvard T-shirt I was wearing while filling up my tank.

These are funny stories about identity and relationships. There is a bit of condescension in assuming that I must be something other than black American if I am also intelligent and high-achieving. But I rarely take these as insults. People like to project the best of themselves onto others. This is especially true when the people are economically vulnerable like the tennis player and the Massachusetts gas attendant. Even when it feels dirty, it mostly comes from a place of pride. And one needs a lot of pride in their culture when they leave it for greener pastures. No matter why you leave, home is still home. And nothing is better than home.

I am much more insulted by the assumption among similarly classed people that I should jump at the chance to be a special kind of black. At a tea party once, a light-skinned black woman fixed her sights on me over a second cup of Earl Grey. She looked like so many of this kind of woman look. She was impeccably styled. Her hair was not chemically treated. The big, frizzy curls marked her as black. The hair may have been at war with the freckles across her nose. In case the hair was not enough, she had chosen some jewelry that, when I remarked upon it, she breezily said was made by a rural woman's collective in Uganda. She had picked it up on her last trip to "the continent." People do not talk like that where I come from. But I have manners. I nodded like it was a perfectly sensible thing to say in response to a perfectly mundane comment. "And you? Did you meet the hostess in Cape Verde?" No, I had not. I have never been to Cape Verde, the small creole African island. "You could say it, you know. There are dark people there like you."

Well, thank you very much.

Cape Verde sounds lovely and I intend to never live there in my life. I told her as much. She never did accept that I was serious. Instead she seemed almost embarrassed for me, so much promise and too ignorant or self-conscious to jump at the chance to be a fake Cape Verdean.

My social status necessitated that I perform or at least desire a different kind of blackness. Often, people seem insulted that I could choose to affect some other version of myself but do not. This desire for a new kind of black pops up in our politics, when we want Barack Obama to be black *and* biracial *and* immigrant *and* black ethnic. Every so often there is a flare-up in popular culture when someone identified as black-black is actually black ethnic. Just like the university context primed these tensions in my life, the context of media and politics produces these conflicts. There is a belief floating around that there is a limited amount of media space held for "black issues," which we often interpret as jobs held by black people. That is true to some extent. Despite our new twenty-four-hour, on-demand, issue-driven media landscape, most outlets allocate a small percentage of their resources to covering anything "black." You can see it in the many talented writers and journalists and analysts who are quarantined in the "race desks" at major media companies.

On occasion, a voice breaks through the social-media-driven discourse. Luvvie Ajayi is a blogger who became a *New York Times* best-selling author, in part because of her commentary on race and gender. Luvvie's career is interesting for many reasons. She figured out the formula for generating real income in a new media landscape where there are more broke famous people than there are genuine celebrities. Her work mixes humor and critique and inspiration. She is younger and far less self-serious than Chimamanda Ngozi Adichie. And she has been touched by god: Oprah Winfrey has endorsed her as an "it" girl. She is, according to one journalist, a "life guru" who is like "Oprah before them."

In 2017 Luvvie poked the social media nest when she

wrote that some black activists try to profit from white guilt. It is a long, drawn-out messy affair with almost no real stakes involved. I'll spare you the details. What is important to understand is that Luvvie had not said anything that has not been said millions of times before by other people for at least a hundred years. W.E.B. DuBois once accused Booker T. Washington of working the white guilt of wealthy patrons for his own personal gain. This is an old slam.

Except Luvvie is Nigerian American. She is black, but the questions arose online and in print, is she black-black? The issue was another old one: who can speak legitimately about and for black people in the United States? For the record, there is no answer. At least there is no good answer. Because the truth is, black people can rarely gatekeep the boundaries of blackness. That is why the artist formerly known as a white woman, Rachel Dolezal, drove so many black people mad. Dolezal had not only presented herself as a black woman. She had not only adopted our hairstyles, our culture, and our struggle as her own. She had done so and there was nothing that black people could do about it.

Dolezal did not need to convince black people that she was black. She only had to convince white people.

I watched another great black voice, Melissa Harris-Perry, give a whole hour to Dolezal on her MSNBC show. Harris-Perry appeared to be indulging Dolezal's performance as legitimate. I have always been certain that this is when Harris-Perry's show lost many of its most hardcore fans: black women. We do not take lightly that we are so vulnerable to the whims of white fancy that we cannot even keep a black woman from lifting up a white woman cosplaying us for personal gain.

Over and over again in research literature on such things, back when black people were not over, we find that the perception of scarcity exacerbates conflicts over who is legitimately black. That is why I would go most of my life having never heard "Where are you from?" until I entered the white, white hallowed halls of Emory University, where we were once told, in all earnestness, that they could not accept more than one black student per year in our department's doctoral program. Scarcity. When Barack Obama was elected, almost every media outlet had to at least perform a nonwhite perspective. For a while, what some people have called "race whisperers" had a steady presence on TV, on mastheads, and in bylines. When Obama left office, black was over. And so was the race and culture desk at MTV News, among others. Scarcity.

When there is only room for a few blacks there is a competition for which black should prevail. That is also what my colleagues were saying to me that day as we sat around debating the merits of a student's research project. There is only so much attention to go around, and if the question is going to be about race or racism, then black people have had more than their fair share of attention. We had resolved the issue of the negro problem, and the negro was the problem. It was time to move beyond that "black-white dichotomy," by which it was meant that we had exhausted all valuable social inquiry into black life. If resources are scarce, then black is over.

The comment was not all that unique. It remains strange that it was said to me, specifically. Initially, I took it as an invitation and would forcefully refuse it: "No, I am not from anywhere special. I am just black." Then I tried taking it as a misguided but well-meaning attempt at solidarity. As in, we are all in this anti-whiteness, anti-colonialism thing together, but I cannot say that I am black so let's pretend that you aren't either. Eventually I decided that asking me to be something other than black, exchanging black for being a person of color was anything but well-meaning. Finally, for now, I have decided on being as black-black as I can be. It is my protest.

If you think that I am intelligent and ambitious and reasoned and formidable, if you think one good thing about me at all, then I insist that you reconcile that with me just being regular black-black. My mother once paid for a coach to help me lose my southern accent. I can still do it, if I think about it hard enough. You basically wake up your tongue; by nature southern tongues are lazy, like our summers. You get the tongue to stand up straight and you flatten the back of the mouth just a bit. That will take out about 60 to 70 percent of your southernness. The rest is about syntax and meter. Strangely enough, to de-southern speech is often to whiten your speech. I could do it, but I do not want to.

I will not code switch on NPR or *The Daily Show with Trevor Noah* or at the White House. I do not do it in front of my students or with the young people in my life. I do not want to be unattainable for these people that I love. Doing that requires a lot of work on my ego. I have to constantly sacrifice the idea of scarcity. I know scarcity is mostly a social construction, but it is something else entirely to act like I know. No one can speak to a singular black experience, not even me. Especially not me. Rejecting that belief does not free me, but it goes a long way toward being authentic.

Black is not over. The postcolonial project of dismantling the vestiges of imperialism is about blackness, just like the U.S. Civil War was about slavery. There is no post-black race theory or race work or racial justice or activism that can thrive by avoiding this truth. Whether at a dinner table or in grand theories, the false choice between black-black and worthy black is a trap. It poses that ending blackness was the goal of anti-racist work when the real goal has always been and should always be ending whiteness.

The Price of
Fabulousness

Fabulousness doesn't take a lot of money. It requires high levels of creativity, imagination and originality; it's dangerous, political, risky, and largely practiced by queer, trans, transfeminine people of color or other marginalized groups; it's about making a spectacle of oneself in a world that seeks to suppress and undervalue fabulous people.

—madison moore, "Fabulousness"[1]

What do you call an educated negro with a B.A. or an M.A., with a B.S., or a Ph.D.? You call him a nigger.

—Malcolm X[2]

Everybody needs a crew. I have many because I am embarrassingly fortunate. One of my crews gathers sporadically to discuss culture, politics, or economics when something in the zeitgeist is especially interesting to us. Jamelle Bouie is a political editor at Slate magazine. Gene Demby is a co-host of the NPR podcast Code Switch when he is not writing, producing, and running distances better left driven. And the mastermind behind it all is Aisha Harris, writer and producer (also at Slate). In the twilight of Barack Obama's presidency, black writers and pundits and thinkers were tired. Many of us had powered through what felt like countless videos of black men and women being executed by the police. We had watched or felt or experienced *the civil unrests in Ferguson and Baltimore and Charlotte. We had marched in New York and Atlanta and Chicago and Oakland and Boston. We reported on and analyzed Hillary Clinton and Bernie Sanders. And then we watched our colleagues and intellectual ballasts rationalize Donald Trump, dismiss our expertise, and mock our concerns that he could win.*

What had been called "the race beat" in the 1960s was just as exhausting and demoralizing in 2016. A joke among those of us who study race is that we never get to move beyond 101, because the world around us is always stuck in first gear.

Our crew wanted out of first gear. In 2018 we sat down to discuss the Starbucks Incident. It is now part of the year in social media clips of white people calling the police on black people for merely existing.[3] There was the Starbucks manager who called the police on the black male patrons who did not buy a cup of coffee quickly enough for her liking. Alison Ettel did not like the young black girl who was selling cold waters on a hot day on a public sidewalk, so she pretended to call the police on her. Some black folks in Oakland decided to BBQ in the park (because out west they don't know the difference between a BBQ and a cookout, but I digress). Jennifer Schulte, a white woman, called the police on them for using charcoal grills after reportedly tossing around the word nigger.

A twelve-year-old boy in Ohio started a grass-cutting business. A white woman thought he had cut too close to her yard, so she called the police on him. A black man was listening to a Bikram yoga CD in his car before a class when a white woman called the police on him for making it hard for her to live. A black family in North Carolina bought a home in a community with a pool—no small feat given the decline in black homeownership after the Great Recession. One of their neighbors promptly called the police on them when they used it. It's a genre.

Throughout the public discussions about "white people calling the cops on black people who are just living" is the idea that black people were, in almost all of these cases, buying something. Or they had rightfully bought something: a house, a meal, a cup of coffee. People made many appeals to the right of consumption. Americans have the right to buy! It is a tenuous right indicative of our consumer society. Being a consumer, or not, should not condition your civil rights. That kind of thinking is how we end up with cruel policies that police where homeless people can sit in public or where poor people can stand without violating an ordinance. The idea is also ridiculous for how it ignores the history of black people buying wrong. Like many ideas about race, these notions are contradictory and yet live side by side in our popular imagination.

Black people deserve to consume in peace, but also, black people consume wrong. Compounding the complexity is the assumption that most black people are poor. Not only are black people wasteful, but they are poor and wasteful. Indeed, our poor consumption patterns are often offered up as the reason why we are more likely to be poor. The following essay was written a few years before the crew sat down to talk about the crisis of black consumption in white spaces. But it is part of that story.

Every time there is a national news story about a black shopper harassed in a store, there is a predictable backlash to the miscarriage of justice. We tend to move quickly from being outraged that it happened to critiquing why a black person was shopping there at all. Much as we interrogate what a woman was wearing when she was raped, we look for ways to assign personal responsibility for structural injustices to bodies we collectively do not value. If you are poor, why do you spend money on useless status symbols like handbags and belts and clothes and shoes and televisions and cars? One thing I've learned is that one person's illogical belief is another person's survival skill. And nothing is more logical than trying to survive.

My family is a classic black American migration family. We have rural southern roots, moved north, and almost all have returned. I grew up watching my great-grandmother, and later my grandmother and mother, use our minimal resources to help other people make ends meet. We were those good poors, the kind who live mostly within our means. We had a little luck when a male relative got extra military pay when he came home a paraplegic or used the VA to buy a Jim Walter house.[4] If you were really blessed, when a relative died with a paid-up insurance policy, you might be gifted a lump sum to buy the land that Jim Walter used as collateral to secure your home lease.

That is how generational wealth happens where I am from: lose a leg, a part of your spine, die right, and maybe you can lease-to-own a modular home. We had a little of that kind of rural black wealth, so we were often in a position to help folks less fortunate. But perhaps the greatest resource we had was a bit more education.

We were big readers and we encouraged the girl children, especially, to go to some kind of college. Consequently, my grandmother and mother had a particular set of social resources that helped us navigate mostly white bureaucracies to our benefit. We could, as my grandfather would say, talk like white folks. We loaned that privilege out a lot. I remember my mother taking a next-door neighbor down to the social service agency. The elderly woman had been denied benefits to care for the granddaughter she was raising. Her denial had come in the genteel bureaucratic way—lots of waiting, forms, and deadlines she could not quite navigate. I watched my mother put on her best Diana Ross *Mahogany* outfit: a camel-colored cape with matching slacks and knee-high boots. I was miffed, as only an only child could be, about sharing my mother's time with the neighbor girl. I must have said something about why we had to do this. The Vivian fixed me with a stare as she was slipping on her pearl earrings and told me that people who can do, must do.

It took half a day, but something about my mother's performance of respectable black person—her Queen's English, her *Mahogany* outfit, her straight bob and pearl earrings—got done what the elderly lady next door had not been able to get done in over a year. I learned, watching my mother, that there was a price we had to pay to signal to gatekeepers that we were worthy of engaging. It meant dressing well and speaking well. It might not work. It likely wouldn't work, but on the off chance that it would, you had to try. It was unfair, but, as The Vivian always said, "Life isn't fair, little girl."

I internalized that lesson and I think it has worked out for me, if unevenly. A woman at Belk once refused to show me the Dooney & Bourke purse I was interested in buying. The Vivian once made a salesgirl cry after she ignored us in an empty store. I have walked away from many a hotly desired purchase, like the impractical off-white winter coat I desperately wanted, after some bigot at the counter insulted me and my mother. But I have a Ph.D. and I support myself by aping the white male privileged life of the mind. It's a mixed bag. Of course, the trick is you can never know the counterfactual of your life. There is no evidence of access denied. Who knows what I was not granted for not enacting the right status behaviors or symbols at the right time for an agreeable authority?

Respectability rewards are a crapshoot, but we do what we can within the limits of the constraints imposed by a complex set of structural and social interactions designed to limit access to status, wealth, and power. I do not know how much my mother spent on her camel-colored cape or knee-high boots, but I know that whatever she paid was returned in hard-to-measure dividends. How do you put a price on the double-take of a clerk at the welfare office who decides you might not be like those other trifling women in the waiting room and provides an extra bit of information about completing a form that you would not have known to ask about? What is the retail value of a school principal who defers a bit more to your child, because your mother's presentation of self signals that she might unleash the bureaucratic savvy of middle-class parents to advocate for her child? I didn't know the price of these critical engagements with organizations and gatekeepers relative to our poverty when I was growing up. But I am living proof of its investment yield.

Why do poor people make stupid, illogical decisions to buy status symbols? For the same reason all but only the most wealthy buy status symbols, I suppose. We want to belong. And not just for the psychic rewards, but belonging to one group at the right time can mean the difference between unemployment and employment, a good job as opposed to a bad job, housing or a shelter, and so on. Someone mentioned on Twitter that poor people can be presentable with affordable options from Kmart. But the issue is not about being presentable.

Presentable is the bare minimum of social civility. It means being clean, not smelling, wearing shirts and shoes for service, and the like. Presentable as a sufficient condition for gainful, dignified work or successful social interactions is a privilege. It's the aging white hippie who can cut the ponytail of his youthful rebellion and walk into senior management, while aging Black Panthers can never completely outrun the effects of stigmatization against which they were courting a revolution. Presentable is relative and, like life, it ain't fair. In contrast, "acceptable" is about gaining access to a limited set of rewards granted upon group membership.

A manager at the apartment complex where I worked while in college told me, repeatedly, that she knew I was "okay" because my little Nissan was clean. That I had worn a Jones New York suit to the interview really sealed the deal. She could call the suit by name, because she asked me about the label in the interview. Another hiring manager at my first professional job looked me up and down in the waiting room, cataloging my outfit, and later told me that she had decided I was too classy to be on the call center floor. I was hired as a trainer instead. The difference meant no shift work, greater prestige, better pay, and a baseline salary for all my future employment.

I have about a half dozen other stories like this. What is remarkable is not that this happened. There is empirical evidence that women and people of color are judged by their appearances differently and more harshly than are white men. What is remarkable is that these gatekeepers, in one way or another, actually told me why I was deemed acceptable. They wanted me to know how I had properly signaled that I was not a typical black or a typical woman, two identities that in combination are almost always conflated with being poor.

I sat in on an interview for a new administrative assistant once. My regional vice president was doing the hiring. A long line of mostly black and brown women applied because we were a cosmetology school. Trade schools at the margins of skilled labor in a gendered field are necessarily classed and raced. I found one candidate particularly charming. She was trying to get out of a salon because ten hours on her feet cutting hair would average out to an hourly rate below minimum wage. A desk job with forty set hours and medical benefits represented mobility for her. When she left, my VP turned to me and said, "Did you see that tank top she had on under her blouse?! OMG, you wear a silk shell, not a tank top!" Both of the women were black. The VP had constructed her job as senior management. She drove a brand-new

BMW because she "should treat herself," and liked to tell us that ours was an image business. A girl wearing a cotton tank top as a shell was incompatible with BMW-driving VPs in the image business.

Gatekeeping is a complex job of managing boundaries that do not just define others but also define ourselves. Status symbols—silk shells, designer shoes, luxury handbags—become keys to unlock these gates. If I need a job that will save my lower back and move my baby from Medicaid to an HMO, how much should I spend signaling to people like my former VP that I will not compromise her status by opening the door to me? Maybe that candidate could not afford a proper shell. I will never know. But I do know that had she gone hungry for two days to pay for it or missed wages for a trip to the store to buy it, she may have been rewarded a job that could have lifted her above minimum wage. Shells aren't designer handbags, perhaps. But a cosmetology school in a strip mall isn't a job at Bank of America, either.

At the heart of incredulous statements about the poor decisions poor people make is a belief that we, the hard-working, sensible not-poor, would never be like them. We would know better. We would know to save our money, eschew status symbols, cut coupons, practice puritanical sacrifice to amass a million dollars. There is a regular news story of a lunch lady who, unbeknownst to all who knew her, dies rich and leaves it all to a cat or a charity or some such. Books about the modest lives of the rich like to tell us how they drive Buicks instead of BMWs. What we forget, if we ever knew, is that what we know now about status and wealth creation and sacrifice are predicated on who we are—that is, not poor.

If you change the conditions of your not-poor status, you change everything you know as a result of being a not-poor. You have no idea what you would do if you were poor until you are poor. And not intermittently poor or formerly not-poor, but born poor, expected to be poor, and treated by bureaucracies, gatekeepers, and well-meaning respectability authorities as inherently poor. Then, and only then, will you understand the relative value of a ridiculous status symbol to someone who intuits that they cannot afford to not have it.

Black Girlhood,
Interrupted

Black girlhood studies is about the representations, memories, and lived experiences of being and becoming in a body marked as youthful, Black, and female. Black girlhood is not dependent, then, on age, physical maturity, or any essential category of identity.

—Ruth Nicole Brown[1]

I am attracted to black women's biographies. The first one I remember reading is Anne Moody's autobiography, *Coming of Age in Mississippi*.[2] Moody was a noted civil rights activist, but I did not care nearly as much about that as I did about reading on black girlhood. I was maybe seven years old and spending a summer "up north" with family, as families did to save money on summer childcare. A little girl, especially, had to be supervised. The book was too mature for me, which is exactly as I preferred them. It is full of the violence of Jim Crow and sharecropping and being country poor. My mother often said country poor was different from city poor. Moody's book made plain what my mother meant. I pushed through the challenging parts, the bigger words and references I could not yet parse, all to get to the parts about what it was like for this black woman to be a girl.

It is not easy to read about girls. As a voracious reader, I knew perhaps all of the widely available books. I loved Ramona Quimby, danced with the idea of teenagerdom in Sweet Valley High, and decided I was Claudia in the Baby-Sitters Club. I understood that these were not the books you read in school, but after one had read *The Diary of Anne Frank*, school reading was all boys on rafts and men traversing the Canterbury Tales and wicked wives who betray their kings. The first black girl I read in school was in the seventh grade. It was a poem by Nikki Giovanni, still my romantic favorite because it was when I decided that I would write my own poems, my own stories. Until college, if I wanted to read about black girlhood I had to read the life stories of black women. That is what I was searching for at seven years old when I read Anne Moody.

The thing I remember most about reading for black girlhood was that the easiest way to locate the girl in a story about a woman was to search for the sexual trauma. It was always there: a dirty uncle, a mother's new husband, a dotty brother, a mean boy at school, a nasty white man, any nasty man. Being raped, molested, "touched" seemed to be the one thing, other than Jim Crow and beauty salons and spirituals, that hung black womanhood together.

It is certainly what I have in common with Oprah Winfrey and Gabrielle Union and the hundreds of black women who wrote to me when I decided to write about R. Kelly. R. Kelly is a superstar. I was there, living my black girl middle years, when R. Kelly became what we used to call an "urban" radio star. He sang dirty R&B for black young people who needed soul music that was not their parents'. By the 2000s, R. Kelly was an unlikely crossover artist, mostly based on a horrible song in which he believed he could fly. It is just the kind of inspirational, soulless black music that corporations love. It made R. Kelly a safe negro for millions of white consumers. At the same time that R. Kelly was becoming Steve Harvey–fied for mass audiences, his reputation as a sexual predator was solidifying in black communities.

Before the internet, for rumors like the ones I heard about R. Kelly in the 1990s to reach a mid-market, school-age community, they had to travel the hard way. People up north had to tell a cousin on the phone down south who told their friends who reveled in being the ones with the celebrity gossip at vacation Bible school and weekend sleepovers. I heard it from a cousin, a boy who was in his fourth or fifth rap group. No woman in his family would ever be left alone with R. Kelly as long as he had something to say about it. Mind you, no one we were related to was at risk of running into R. Kelly, least of all me. But that is how news was delivered, with equal parts self-importance and public service. R. Kelly liked to touch young girls and we all knew it.

Strangely, it was the same cousin who had told me a few years earlier which black girls deserved what they got. It was over a plate of ribs at my aunt's dining room table that I learned that being a woman is about what men are allowed to do to you. I was fourteen years old. Mike Tyson was the most famous boxer in the world.

For the black people I knew, he was the pinnacle of the black sports elite. He had been born poor and worked his way to riches and fame. But it was 1992 and he had just been found guilty of raping an eighteen-year-old named Desiree Washington in a hotel.

"Y'all act like she's a woman," my cousin said. "She is— excuse me, Auntie—a ho."

That's what I remember most, next to the ribs. My cousin was defending a convicted rapist to a room full of black women, all but one related to him. The elder women shook their heads. The elder men left the room, knowing a fool's errand when they saw one unfolding.

My cousin was feeling himself. Young and approaching fatherhood, he stood his ground. Desiree Washington was a ho, bringing down a black man who had made it.

"What was she doing in the hotel room?" he asked.

"She could have been butt naked in that room and it shouldn't matter," I replied.

He explained how I was different from Ms. Washington mainly by telling me that she was a ho, and implying that I was not a ho by what he left unsaid. There are hoes and then there are women. As a teenager I could go either way. But as a relative I could go only one way: I would not be a ho.

I was not angry, but I was hurt.

"What if your girlfriend is pregnant right now with your daughter?" I asked. "A girl?"

"No daughter of mine would be raised to go to a hotel room. I ain't raising no ho."

It was then that I learned that black girls like me can never truly be victims of sexual predators. And that the men in my life were also men in the world. Men can be your cousin, men can be Mike Tyson, and men can be both of them at the same time.

That resonated with me more recently, as new accusations against R. Kelly emerged in 2017. For decades, he has faced various allegations of child molestation, sexual violence, and abuse (in 2008 in Chicago, for instance, he was found not guilty of child pornography charges). The 2017 firestorm involves the families of two young women who have accused Mr. Kelly of holding their daughters against their will, an accusation one of the women vehemently denies.

Whether or not the accusations are true, R. Kelly's history with women is still soul-crushing: He surreptitiously married the singer Aaliyah when she was fifteen. He admitted to having had sexual relations with young women whose age he cannot or will not verify. And he has portrayed himself as a Svengali too likable to be a sexual predator. As we once did around our big family table, millions of his fans colluded in that portrayal.

I was older when R. Kelly became the sexual predator du jour. Still, I heard the stories. I lived in Chicago for a year in the early 2000s, and the rumors were everywhere. I heard about the McDonald's near a middle school where he supposedly liked to troll for young women and the friend of a friend at work who knew an underage girl who had "dated" him.

I remember the stories about Aaliyah. I fought with

friends, men I adored and respected, when videotapes of R. Kelly having sex with what appeared to be an underage girl were being peddled on street corners.

At a house party, the men laughed when I announced I didn't want us to watch the video, but they finally acquiesced when I displayed the telltale signs of female rage. It was as if a "crazy woman" was a fair reason not to watch child pornography, but my request was not. Never mind respect for the child. I still remember the one guy whose comment about the girl on the cover of the videotape cut through the nervous laughter.

"Look at that body. She almost ready," he said.

What would it take for a black girl to be a victim? I still do not know, but I know what I have been told by men who love me deeply. My friends told me that once they desired you, then you could not be a victim. My cousin said once you were a ho, you could not be a victim. I already knew all of these things by the time I was married, but still it was my father who taught me best of all.

He was in the hospital with a case of the poors. You don't manage your diabetes because someone on the block will pay you for the test strips, you go to the hospital with the poors. You cannot get all of your blood pressure pills because you split them with your girlfriend who makes $145 a month too much for the good Medicaid, you go to the hospital with the poors. You rob Peter to pay Paul but Peter is broke too, you go to the hospital with the poors.

My father was a big man. He was loud and gregarious. He was 100 percent invested in capitalism. "If niggas can give it away, they can sell it," he would tell me. Two weeks after I got married, my new husband and I were summoned to the hospital to visit my dad. He was holding court from the bed, directing me and my stepsister on how to handle his affairs. At the time, his main affairs involved one of us going down to the eviction court and telling the judge that he was in the hospital. Dad wanted an extension on his counter-suit against his landlord, whom he had not paid in a few months. He knew he would lose the case. He wanted only to run down the clock until his new girlfriend's housing voucher came through. Being a poor capitalist is complicated.

What wasn't complicated was what it meant that I was a wife. He had not made it to the wedding. We had eloped, which should have told me something that I was too distracted to notice. This was his first look at my husband. They bonded over their shared careers in television. Pleased, my dad turned to me and said, "Just so you know, if he ever beats you, I won't just take your word for it. There are two sides to every story." To my mind, husband beating and husband raping are right next to each other on the Richter scale of fucked-up things men you trust can do to you. I took it to mean what my cousin once meant—black girlhood ends whenever a man says it ends.

Two sides to every story. Almost ready. She a ho.

Those are the kind of comments I have heard hundreds, if not thousands, of times, from men and women, to excuse violence against black women and girls. If one is "ready" for what a man wants from her, then by merely existing she has consented to his treatment of her. Puberty becomes permission.

All women in our culture are subject to this kind of violence, when people judge their bodies to decide if they deserve abuse. But for black women and girls, that treatment is specific to our history as much as it is about today's context. New research corroborates what black women have long known: people across gender and race see black girls as more adultlike than their white peers. In her book *Pushout*, Monique W. Morris shows that teachers and administrators don't give black girls the care and protection they need. Left to navigate school by themselves because they are "grown," these girls are easily manipulated by men.[3]

The presumption of childhood is not only that you are off-limits to adult desires, but that should an adult violate you, the penalties will account for your structural innocence. But, for black girls, the presumption of innocence is gossamer, at best. One of the few surveys of public attitudes about black girls was conducted in 2014.[4] The majority of those surveyed said that black girls need less protection and nurturing than white girls. Being perceived as grown comes with consequences even when you are not yet an adult.

Those consequences are far-reaching. When a black girl

is perceived by those in her immediate social sphere as "ready," the legal system reinforces that she was ready when it sees her through the expectations of an adult. And we know how little concern the legal system has for women who report sexual assault. Women have the burden of proving not only their assault, but that they did not deserve to be assaulted. The former is bad enough. How do you prove the penetration was forced in the hours after you are emotionally traumatized? Or that you weren't drunk or high? Or that you said no before he started but not while he was "finishing"?[5]

Women have found it nearly impossible to meet the burden of proof. But what if you have proof of violence on your body but the protocols for seeing them systematically erase them? That is the potential of domestic violence protocols that rely on photographic evidence to corroborate a woman's claim in court. The cameras used in criminal domestic violence cases are supposed to document the bruises thought typical of getting one's ass beaten. In a quest to be "evidence-based," a nurse is only allowed to call a spot on a battered woman's body a bruise if it can be seen with the naked eye. What if your skin is too dark to show the bruises that the police often require to believe that you were abused?[6] For black women, a camera designed not to see our abuse becomes a protocol that will only label such spots "dark."

There are many what-ifs for women to prove that they have been sexually assaulted. And each of them fails most women, but they fail black women as if by design. Like the cameras that cannot see and the protocols that will not name, the what-ifs just barely work when the woman involved has the possibility of innocence. That is something black women rarely have, and black girls are thrust into that structural vulnerability younger than their non-black peers.

When adults say that black girls, not yet adults, are more knowledgeable about sex than their white female peers, they are saying that a girl child is responsible for all the desires that adults project onto her. She does not need the protection of childhood, for she has never been a child. This system of neglect and abuse is mostly ignored in social and education policy, because the violence is often sexual and it happens to girls whom society views as disposable. We rarely focus on how programs are failing black women and girls, or how we could intervene to help.

When President Barack Obama created a task force for young black men in 2014, it took months of demands by black women for a similar task force to be created for young black women. Even then, the girls' task force did not receive equal attention or funding.

Watching men I love turn a girl into a woman and a woman into a ho has never left me. That conversation at my aunt's dinner table was not the first time I felt deeply afraid, but it left a cut that will never heal. It's the kind of wound that keeps you alert to every potential doorway through which you might enter as a friend, sister, or woman, but leave as a bitch or a ho.

It is the culture that gives us something like R. Kelly. It is a culture where someone like radio personality Charlamagne Tha God acts as if he is exactly that, a god among mere mortal women who can debate women's right to say no for sport. Charlamagne is just the latest in a string of men I could name that are not Bill Cosby big or who did not assault mostly white women like Harvey Weinstein. These men live in the urban enclaves of media culture neighbor-hoods on radio stations and music labels and third-string reality television shows. The names sound like a place I might go for a good time: Power 105, Hip Hop Divas, *The Source*. These are the places Me Too cannot reach. In these corners black men are too oppressed to also oppress. They are too easily jailed, imprisoned, invisibilized in a prison industrial complex to be batterers or rapists. They made it and we are collectively responsible for lifting them up.

If R. Kelly is our culture's pied piper, then Charlamagne is a bit like our court jester. He is from Moncks Corner, South Carolina, a place I actually know more than a lit-tle bit. It is country and black and southern and hard to make it out of. Charlamagne is not particularly talented, except in his willingness to be seen. He translated that into a successful career on urban radio and the equivalent of Off-Off-Broadway cable television. He made it.

Along the way Charlamagne has played with the rumor that he is also a rapist. In interviews he talks casually about "beating the case." The case in question is that of a fifteen-year-old girl who claims she was drugged and raped at a house Charlamagne rented for a party. He beat the case. But he did not let that make him shy about critiquing the veracity of rape culture. He has, at different times, admitted to "fucking" a woman too drunk to consent, "smashing" while high on drugs, and "taking that pussy." I'm no prude. I, in fact, curse like a sailor. I'm not particularly dismayed at the language about sexual intercourse. It is precisely because I am familiar with what it means to say you smashed that I can look through the words and to the context.

Charlamagne's comments are mundane in the world of barbershop talk and beauty shop talk and corner talk and lunch room talk for millions of black people who have grown up on hip-hop culture. It isn't Charlamagne smashing that should concern us. It is what he will admit to even as he denies ever having raped a woman. Take for instance how he says he "beat" that rape charge of a fifteen-year-old girl:

> I rented a cabin at a place called Short Stay on Nearby Lake Moultrie and invited a whole gang of people to come over and party. . . . The

night started off great—lots of drinking, smoking, dancing, and bullshitting. But at some point one of the girls passed out and when she woke up later that night, she claimed that some of the dudes at the party had sexually assaulted her. I wasn't there at the time—I'd left to go get some weed—and when I finally heard about what had happened, the entire party had cleared out.[7]

Then-twenty-two-year-old Charlamagne will admit to having parties where fifteen-year-old girl guests are presumably so normal as not to have caused any alarm. He will admit he was getting everybody high for some bullshitting. And, while he maintains he did not rape anyone, Charlamagne cannot fathom why someone would think that he would. If a girl was there she must have been ready.

That is the same line R. Kelly is toeing. After years of near silence, in 2018 R. Kelly released a nineteen-minute song called, I kid you not, "I Admit." Like Charlamagne, it isn't so much what R. Kelly denies doing, but what he is comfortable admitting—as defense—to having done:

I admit I fuck with all the ladies, that's both

older and young ladies (ladies, yeah)

But tell me how they call it pedophile because

that shit is crazy (crazy)

You may have your opinions, entitled to your

opinions (opinions)

But really am I supposed to go to jail or lose my

career because of your opinion [. . .]

But this is my advice to you 'cause I'm also a

parent (parent)

Don't push your daughter in my face, and tell

me that it's okay (my face, okay)

'Cause your agenda is to get paid, and get mad

when it don't go your way (yeah, [your] way)

What R. Kelly will admit to is liking the ladies young. He will admit to branding some of them because they like it. He will admit to maybe marrying a teenager at one time. But he thinks we go too far with this whole rape thing. As with Charlamagne, who will smash as you're passed out or pay for the weed that gets the fifteen-year-old party guest too high to consent, one has to wonder what would qualify as rape for the urban radio pied piper and court jester.

For me, as a noncelebrity, it was easy to discern in the black women's stories I loved that what did not qualify as rape was anything done to a black girl. When I went looking for stories about black girls like me, the easiest way to find them was to look for the door, the moment when a black woman had been someone's ho. Almost without fail it is there in every black woman's story. Given that racial segregation persists in our most intimate dwellings—our homes and our families—black women most often cross the threshold when pushed by a black man.

Sexual violence against black girls and women has, until very recently, been hidden in the statistics about "women" writ large. In many ways, those stores are similar. We are most vulnerable to the men in our homes. We are taught to blame ourselves. We fear reprisal for speaking up. But black women and girls face additional burdens of protecting the reputations of black boys and men. As black feminists have argued, that burden has trapped us in cultural silences that a focus on gender violence alone cannot capture.

People of color are similarly hypervigilant when we navigate a white social world. We screen our jokes, our laughter, our emotions, and our baggage. We constantly manage complex social interactions so we are not fired, isolated, misunderstood, miscast, or murdered. We can come home, if we're lucky enough to have a home, and turn off that setting. We often do, as I once did, look for versions of ourselves in literature and pop culture.

But for black girls, home is both refuge and where your most intimate betrayals happen. You cannot turn off that setting. It is the dining room at your family's house, served with a side of your uncle's famous ribs. Home is where they love you until you're a ho.

Girl 6

It would be silly to suggest that people do not understand the importance of good ethos. However, it is not unwise to ask how individuals come to have good ethos. Do speakers have good ethos, because they speak well? Write well? Is there a general assumption that some racial groups have a supposed better ethos than others do? Regrettably, the answer to the latter question is yes. Unfortunately, in the history of race relations in America, black Americans' ethos ranks low among other racial and ethnic groups in the United States. More often than not, their moral characters have been associated with a criminalized and sexualized ethos in visual and print culture. Consequently, assigning black women characteristics associated with good ethos in a slave and post-slavery society has been problematic.

—Coretta Pittman[1]

S ometime in the winter of 2017 I started making a fuss on Twitter. They call that being on-brand. Regardless, I wanted a black woman to have a job as an opinion writer at a prestige publication. It is a silly wish. In the grand scheme of things a black woman op-ed writer at the *New York Times* or the *Washington Post* does not mean much of anything. It will not stop ICE from locking babies in cages. It will not house a family priced out of the community where they have grown up. It isn't a civil rights victory or about Negro Firsts. It will not bring back the Voting Rights Act or impeach Trump or free Palestine or eradicate student loan debt or any of those really important things. Like many things, I wanted it because I wanted it.

Also like many things that I want simply because I want, I had a reason that seemed good enough to me, but one I did not feel compelled to share. This happens when I have kept my own counsel and can anticipate that my reasons will not find a curious audience. I had been keeping my counsel on this particular issue ever since David Brooks wrote 865 words about how gourmet sandwiches are ruining America in the New York effing *Times*.[2] That was 593 words more than the Gettysburg Address and about 365 words more than we allow poor students to write about their neediness on many scholarship applications. These are unfair comparisons, of course. The genre of opinion writing is precisely about this—750 to 1,000 words on something mundane that is secretly profound. If I wanted to be excessively fair, I have foisted upon you an entire volume loosely in that genre. If there is any difference, it is that I try really hard not to write dumb things. I cannot speak for Mr. Brooks.

And the point is about that: I cannot speak for Mr. Brooks and Mr. Brooks cannot speak for me. He is absolutely within his right to wax poetic about how soppressata is synecdoche for growing class divides in the United

States. That is presumably what he was doing in that essay, by the way. His job is to go to lunch at a local fancy sandwich shop with a woman from the office who only has a high school degree that did not cover the pronunciation of *pomodoro*. After which time he is tasked with making such a mundane exchange meaningful to the rest of us, whether we eat take-out chicken pomodoros or make our own basic sandwiches.

The op-ed writer's job is to make their take work for me even if I do not share their cultural milieu. Failing that, that writer should make me aspire to their cultural milieu. I did not much care for a sandwich at the end of Brooks's essay. Nor was I intrigued by what the sandwich shop metaphor was meant to convey: that upper-middle-class Americans had left everyone else behind. That is a real feat, as I am professionally honor bound to care about class inequality. It is in my job description. Yet I was so bored by the metaphor, and its assumptions about those with high school diplomas being intimidated by deli meat, that by the end I could only think of eating the rich. By that measure the essay failed.

It did not matter that the essay failed. Many of Mr.

Brooks's essays fail, if public mocking is a measure of such things. At least once a month "the latest Brooks" makes the rounds of my admittedly self-satisfied peers. We marvel that the man has a job that qualifies him to be introduced at some fancy dinner as a "public intellectual." And yet, he will have a job. This week and the week after that and the weeks after every bad essay that misses some notable point or reading or data. Mr. Brooks will be back because his job is not to be right but to be there, on the page of your *New York Times*.

For many reasons, well-educated opinion writers like to critique the system of elite higher education that produced their social class. The rest of us in higher education are merely put-upon to live with the stereotypes that feel as foreign to us as David Brooks imagines fancy deli sandwiches feel to most working-class Americans. And that is the rub. I do not get much value from the intellectual class at prestige publications, but as a thinker in public *I have to respond to them*. That is the power of those pages. My friends and I may be smarty pants, but David Brooks is the legitimate intellectual. That is how legitimacy works. After that deli meat flummoxed David Brooks and he saw fit to tell us all about it, I started wondering about what I would tell the world about how I experience its most mundane machinations.

A few months ago I could not get the City of Richmond to give me a trash can. They call them "supercans," which sounds like it has a lot of cool powers but just means it can hold three Amazon Prime boxes. That is good because I am really working on being a socialist black feminist. It would help if my comrades did not see my Amazon Prime boxes in my trash can. As it is, I am careful never to link to my book page on Amazon or take a selfie where you can see the traitorous blue tag in the background. I made that book link mistake once on social media and I am still apologizing for not linking to the unionized Powell's bookstore. I wonder if the county that surrounds my city has the same problem getting supercans. The county is white-ish. The city is black-ish. Something tells me that the level of municipal efficiency I am getting in the city versus the county has something to do with that demographic reality. Anyway, I ended up sending an email to the mayor, typed in my white voice, appended with my professional title that also has links to my Powell's book page in my bio. They brought me a can and one for my neighbor to boot. That's the kind of thing I might talk about.

Or there is the whole thing I am having about hair weaves lately. For years black women's consumption of "fake" hair has been used to mock our inability to meet femme beauty standards, themselves judged by whatever is natural for white women femmes. Forget that hair augmentation is as old as recorded human history, transcends national origin and culture and surely race. Ain't nobody got time for facts when there is a black woman waiting to be a punchline. Anyway, I have been thinking about the political economy of hair weaves. For years East Asian communities dominated in the production and distribution of hair weave across the world. The hair could be had for cheap, but you paid a hefty price with your time. There was driving to the one good store in your town or maybe the town over. There was waiting for weeks for a special delivery or a friend of a coworker's cousin who was driving down to Atlanta and could pick it up for you. For many black people, buying hair in the local beauty supply store is how we experienced immigration—Korean, Chinese, and Vietnamese shopkeepers selling us colonized beauty from the heads of poor women in nations that the West has deliberately kept poor. We wear globalism on our heads.

I thought about that when I found an Amazon link for hair weave. The global middleman that has gobbled up almost every supply chain in the world, from food to shipping containers, was officially in the weave business. Did this mean that Chinese manufacturers were being edged out, or were they leveraging technology? It seemed to me that you could not talk about a hair weave, really talk about it, if you were not also talking about supply chains, currencies, gender, and geopolitics. One man's Italian meat is another woman's Afro-curl 1-B bundles.

You know, those kinds of things. That is what I thought I might talk about if I had carte blanche to talk about any mundane thing for a national readership, with no repercussions for failing to find either accuracy or an audience.

———

That is, I suppose, what I wanted when I wanted what I want: a black woman somewhere in this world to have the freedom to be banal as a matter of course for her job. I wanted her to be well compensated, protected, and free to fail. I wanted one woman who might touch a comb I use or walk a block I travel to talk about anything her heart desired for a publication where whatever is said matters, by default.

As has been mentioned, this thing I wanted was not a big deal in the grand scheme of things. That is why I took to Twitter to complain. That is where one goes to complain about things that are officially Not a Big Deal. People responded because, again, it is Not a Big Deal and in the age of social media the rate of opinions is inversely proportional to importance. People threw out names of black women who write for prestige publications: Roxane Gay, Melissa Harris-Perry, Brittney Cooper, and a handful of others. All wonderful women . . . who have day jobs. They are professors and researchers and teachers and authors. They run research centers and media companies and nonprofits. They write for the *Times* or the *Post* as their fourth- or fifth-shift job. I love black women too much to ever wish for us another part-time job. I had been clear. I wanted a full-time, flat-out sinecure with a black woman in it.

More opinions rolled in. The women at *The Undefeated* and *Cosmo* and Shondaland.com and *Teen Vogue* are doing amazing things, they said. We outchea. Well, yeah, I know we outchea. That was my point. I could name three dozen black women off the top of my head who have the talent for such a position *at a prestige publication*.[3] That last bit mattered. Saying why it matters is one of those sticky things about my work. We do not share much in the U.S. culture of individualism except our delusions about meritocracy. God help my people, but I can talk to hundreds of black folks who have been systematically separated from their money, citizenship, and personhood and hear at least eighty stories about how no one is to blame but themselves. That is not about black people being black but about people being American. That is what we do. If my work is about anything it is about making plain precisely how prestige, money, and power structure our so-called democratic institutions so that most of us will always fail. That is what my book *Lower Ed* is fundamentally about.[4] It is what all of my work is about.

In media as in higher education, we need to believe that all publications matter. And they do, to someone somewhere. But, for good or for ill, elite publications are still a thing. I am very amenable to the idea that perhaps they should not be a thing. But wishing don't make it so. Reality matters.

The reality is that for writers, there are few gigs as good as those at publications where they have the freedom and protection to write well. Writing well takes research assistance, editorial expertise, copyeditors, lunch breaks, fresh air, desk space, peers, and LexisNexis subscriptions. Writing is democratic. Writing well is not.

You know who knows this is true? Writers at nonprestige publications. They love their freedom. They may love their publication's mission. But I know a lot of writers, and few of them would agree that their work would not benefit from the kind of wealth that accompanies the prestige of the publications that we all complain about.

If your job does not afford you that stability, you are lucky if your family can make up the slack. There are a lot of media people who are so lucky. That is why the first, best criteria for most entry-level jobs in media—especially at prestige media companies—is a family wealthy enough to afford you the unpaid internship you will have to take to get your foot in the door. You know who is statistically, systematically unlikely to have that kind of family wealth? Let's just say it isn't David Brooks.

It is poor people from nonurban centers and first-generation college students and immigrants and the children of some kinds of immigrants and it is black people. That is why the black women's names on the tip of so many tongues were those who had jobs elsewhere. How else could a typical black woman afford to write for free or for cheap?

Sure, I wanted what I wanted for the sister in question, but I also wanted it for the rest of us. While the op-ed pages do not matter to a great deal of important things, that is not the same as them not mattering at all. What happens when David Brooks writes about deli meat as class warfare? In my world, made up of a lot of academics and college graduates and creative types, the link pierces our awareness on social media. Or, because we are by and large those kinds of people, we read it in our *New York Times* home delivery or the app on our phone. Someone sends it to us on one of our listservs. Or, if you work in media, you have to know about it and so you do somehow. It is in the ether. A David Brooks utterance is the ether.

That week, let's say you want to talk about voter suppression or Shonda Rhimes or something other than deli meat. But now the ether has come for your air. You have to contend with the ridiculousness of a David Brooks utterance to get to the thing you want to talk about. You can ignore it, but you risk opting out of the backchannel chatter where status is negotiated. You can be the academic with the book on Iberian ham who gets the call from the writer who was assigned the thankless job of following up on David Brooks's deli meat sandwich. Now you can talk about boutique labor in food processing to no one, which is what your book is really about, or you can talk to lots of people about why poor people are scared of sliced Italian meatstuffs.

None of it matters, but it starts to take on the weight of something that matters, if only for the day or two of the news cycle. You, the serious person, cannot be serious unless or until you engage or affirmatively choose to ignore David Brooks on sandwich meat. That is where we are.

My Twitter rant was a thought experiment. What if one could not be a public intellectual unless or until he or she had engaged or affirmatively chosen to ignore some black woman's thoughts on edge control? What if David Brooks or some of his class compatriots like Jonathan Chait had to entertain a dozen questions about the political economy of wet and wavy before they could move on to their latest thoughts about the death of liberalism? It would not matter to a starving child, but I would find it entertaining.

More than that, it would say who you have to engage to be taken seriously. As being taken seriously becomes a form of reputational capital in a culture where reputation is like the Bitcoin of status cultures, being taken seriously is real work. The royal "we" take our cues about what ideas matter from whom we must recognize before we ourselves can matter. Historically these kinds of fine-grained status distinctions were hard to parse. You sense that there was some mono-culture your own culture brushed up against as you tried to extract what you needed from those around you for your survival and flourishing. The datafication of our reputational currency, how we derive the status we need to maintain the status we have or desire, becomes a bit less opaque.

Take, for instance, who we follow on something like Twitter. Now listen, nothing about Twitter is a stand-in for someone's soul. I follow a porn anime account because sometimes they tweet really neat pictures of black cartoon characters. Only god can judge me. But I am not really an institution. I work for an institution, yet my engagement with the public is not one of my core professional responsibilities. Put another way, I can be a professor with a public, but I do not need a public to be a professor.

On the other hand, media people are people, but they are also institutions. It is a very hard line to draw, but that does not mean that the line is not there or that it should not be drawn. In the same way it matters that Donald Trump cannot now legally block people on Twitter because he occupies the office of the presidency, a reporter at an influential newspaper cannot be entirely separated from their role in the Fourth Estate.[5] A reporter needs a public to be a reporter and, as such, who said reporter is in public is relevant to their job. My anime account issue is more personal than professional. The same is not true of journalists and writers affiliated with major publications.

Who you follow on Twitter in the course of being in public as part of your profession—again, a profession that requires a public—might say a little something about who you must engage to be taken seriously as a professional. If you check out who, say, Melissa Harris-Perry follows on social media you will see an expected mix of people: journalists, academics, writers, public intellectuals, publications' official accounts, and so on. What you will also see is a glimpse into who Melissa Harris-Perry considers a peer or culturally congruent.

Because I am beating up on David Brooks here, I went from Melissa's Twitter follows to his. At first glance it looked like any conclusion I might draw would be dicey. That was a sign that I had better quantify it. And that is what I did. I extracted the name of every one of the 322 accounts that David Brooks followed on a given day. Then I went through and verified that all of those accounts were real, as opposed to parody accounts. Using an algorithm called my brain, I manually cross-referenced the name of every noninstitutional account on the list. Because almost all (except two) of those accounts were of people who are at least marginally public, it was fairly straightforward to determine their racial and gender self-identification.

As others have found when doing similar processes on political leaders, a man on Twitter followed a lot of dudes.[6] Not a huge surprise. But what I wanted to know is if David Brooks listens to any black women, and if he does, who and how many?

Of those 322 accounts, six are black women. Now, black is complex. I wanted to be very generous here. If a woman had any marker anywhere of (1) being African American, (2) being black in America, (3) being of African descent, or (4) having once stood close to the black hair aisle in a Walgreens, I listed her as a black woman. The number is six.

Of the 322 people that a public intellectual chooses to engage however marginally as a professional peer, six are black women.

That may mean something or nothing at all. Important people do not follow a lot of people in social media. It is one of those minute forms of status signaling we do now. A high ratio of followers to followed suggests that you are serious, a leader as opposed to some social media rando. Serious people are not #TeamFollowBack. It is possible, then, that David Brooks only follows ballers. Or, he only followed 300 people when he first signed up for Twitter after someone in the *New York Times* marketing department told him he had to. The follows may be random and meaningless. Or they could be meaningful or anomalous.

No matter what you think, we might agree that it is not fair to pick on David Brooks. I decided to throw in another writer, of similar stature but a different political persuasion. Jonathan Chait is with *New York* magazine. He is a Very Serious Person. On the same day that David Brooks was following 322 people, Jonathan Chait was following 370. Now, Chait's wheelhouse is a bit different from Brooks's. Brooks muses. He is a muser. He muses about cab rides and meat sandwiches and hippie kids these days and what it all means. Chait is mostly a long-form writer who also writes op-eds. His beat, as he rather defensively described it in 2018, is mostly about the decline of western civilization. There is something in there about current politics—Russiagate and what have you—and a dash of political theory about the Enlightenment, and a really serious absolutely-not-weird commitment to exposing the intolerant campus left. It is all very heady stuff.

Whatever their respective genres, Brooks and Chait share this: six. That is also the number of black women Chait follows. Six. It has a magical ring to it. Six is a perfect number because the sum of all of its factors equals six. Six is also the mark of the devil. The six black women on each of Chait's and Brooks's list are exceptional. They are primarily colleagues at their respective institutions or in their profession. At least one has a television program, which could be useful as both Brooks and Chait write books and what have you. I could name thirty-six black women whose musings warrant mundane engagement. Thirty-six. And that is without thinking about it.

Twitter is not especially meaningful as an example of how little engagement professionally smart people do with black women. But that is the beauty of it. When black writers are not read or black thinkers are not cited or black activists are not interviewed, we can say that it is just too hard for those who do not live, work, or learn near black people to find any. It is just so hard. But Twitter is easy. It costs nothing, in either time or money, to engage with someone who won't move into your neighborhood or sit beside you at a dinner party or run into you at the fancy deli. When it is free to do so with little risk to one's reputation or worldview, some of our most well-known opinion writers employed by some of the most legitimate publications do not have to engage with black women in any real capacity to retain their legitimacy.

When the people we read, even if we only read them to hate them, do not engage black women as thinkers or subjects, we do not feel compelled by our dominant culture to do so either. Presumably, a black woman writer is an exception because we all deal with ourselves as subjects, if we do not deal with anyone else. That has been the basis of my professional writing career. I am a black woman thinker for hire, because so few prestige publications hire us, support us, pay us, give us second chances when we are inevitably human, and present us to their readership as necessary to engage if they are to understand the world.

Every black woman I could think of who was writing

op-eds as a regular part of her public intellectual work at a prestige publication was doing so as a second-, third-, and even fourth-shift job. This is what that looks like for me. In my competitive day job I teach, research, write, and administrate. In my second job, I organize and volunteer in my various communities. For women with children, this is usually when they do their yeoman's share of the childrearing. In a few years I look forward to caring for aging parents. On my third shift, I research, write, and publish essays for public audiences on race, racism, gender, sexism, class, classism, education, economics, and culture. Only one of those jobs provides me pay and health insurance. And one of the others potentially jeopardizes that job.

I do that third-shift work for the same reason I do the second-shift work: I believe it matters. Hill Collins calls this critical truth-telling. It speaks to the masses using the discourse of the powerful that affords me the legitimacy to do both. There is certainly more than a bit of personal benefit to doing that work. I am occasionally paid to do it. I generate a kind of status from doing it that can augment my profile as an academic. I also make it easier for publications not to hire a black woman full-time. I give cover to publications that refuse to call racism racist. I receive death threats and hate mail and can never trust social interactions with strangers in public. I am just public enough to be targeted for harassment without many of the attendant benefits of being very well known.

But I also get letters from black girls who tell me that they saw themselves in something I wrote. I get notes from men and women who have reconsidered their beliefs because they read something I wrote. And I embody for many white people, especially those who will never venture far beyond a high-class deli shop to speak to actual people who are very different from them, a view of an unfair and unjust world.

Still, no one has to respond to me. I am not important enough in the stratified world of public intellectualism to command engagement. A Professional Smart Person can be so without ever reading a black woman, ever interviewing a black woman, ever following a black woman, or ever thinking about a black woman's existence. That is why I wanted one—just one—black woman safely ensconced in the hallowed halls of prestige media so that the intelligentsia's cultural critique translates the interests of power into the taken-for-granted beliefs of those who are nowhere near as close to it as they presume they are.

I would not care (much) what that black woman wrote about. David Brooks writes about sandwiches. Thomas Friedman writes about his taxi driver. If a black woman wants to write about the silk head scarf she sleeps in to protect her hair, that would be at least as valuable. I preferred a black woman who was not conservative-for-pay, but I was not even ready to draw that line. Because even such a black woman would necessitate that her peers—mostly white, almost all male, few with any discernible ties to anyone different from themselves—figure out how to treat a black woman as a peer for a public who so rarely sees that happen in any context.

Black women do not have all the answers. We are not superheroes, and ours is not the definitive worldview. But we are trustworthy subjects, of our own experiences and of ways of knowing. One of the more resilient slogans from the social media era of black cultural production is "Trust black women." Sisters on social media say it to make their legitimate claim to what they know about their own experiences. Others, whether in solidarity or because it sounds cool, say it to "check" those who are questioning a black woman's truth claim.

More recently, "Trust black women" even filtered out to mainstream politics. As the Hillary Clinton, Bernie Sanders, and Donald Trump debates were raging during the 2016 presidential election, high-profile women pointed to black women's overwhelming support for Clinton as an indicator of how the Democratic Party should govern. "Trust black women," Linda Sarsour, national co-chair of the Women's March, told her supporters. The idea of trusting black women is intrinsic to my desire to see a black woman on the op-ed pages.

It is not that all or any black woman is beyond reproach, but that she cannot be reproached merely for being a black woman. It is still a radical idea. It is at the heart of my research: black women are rational and human. Working from that assumption, I work my way analytically through political theory, economics, history, sociology, and culture. It rarely fails me.

I thought about this rarity recently. Donald Trump's election had been one thing. There was clearly an aspect of race and gender at play. Women, some of them black, weighed in on what it meant that 53 percent of the white women who voted did so for Trump. But, as Trump's eclectic, manic style of governance set in, public discussion turned to ideas about Russia and fascism and economic anxiety. I understand all of these issues as ones to which black women contribute meaningful analysis.

Black women who think about the liberatory possibilities for black people through forms of governance can surely speak to how we understand Russia in 2018. If Hannah Arendt is the definitive voice on fascism among our intellectual classes, then surely black women who have lived under fascist U.S. policies here and abroad can shed light on our cultural moment. If economic anxiety shapes one's political attitudes, would not a group of voters who have always lived with near-recessionary rates of unemployment and stagnant wages for generations have illuminating thoughts on labor, on the economy? It seemed so to me.

It still seems so to me. In July 2018, the *New York Times*

announced that Michelle Alexander would be joining their stable of regular opinion writers. She is the first woman of color to ever do so.[7] In 2018.

Interestingly enough, as of this writing, Michelle is not one of the six black women on either Brooks's or Chait's list. She is a serious writer who writes seriously about criminalization. She wrote a best-selling book.[8] She is a Heinz Award winner. She is supremely qualified. Perhaps even overqualified, as is generally the case for black women who are, on average, overeducated for their professional positions. She has that in common with the black women on the list of six. None of them can be honestly described as some blogger or an independent iconoclast, which is how we might talk about many white men who wrote their way into the public intellectual ether. There still is not a seriously left-leaning woman of any color or race at these publications. And that is my next complaint. You can catch it on Twitter.

ACKNOWLEDGMENTS

This collection represents conversations I have had with many wonderful communities, some that intersect and others that do not. I have been fortunate. My interlocutors include social theorists, historians, sociologists, anthropologists, writers, researchers, academics, politicians, activists, and readers from all walks of life. They have pushed me to refine my analytical concepts without sacrificing my prose. And they have inspired me to aim for a cohesive framework of thought in our complicated days.

I owe my editor, Tara Grove of The New Press, an immeasurable debt for engaging me seriously, critically, and always in good faith. As a writer and a thinker it is difficult to find people willing to wade into your thought process to throw you a line out of it, which is what one must eventually do to write anything for a public. It is even more rare for a black woman thinker and writer to garner that kind of serious engagement with her intellectual production. I have, quite honestly, spent my entire life trying to find anyone who valued me enough as a thinker to engage me enough that I might become a better one. Tara does that.

Writing is always a brutally social process that is rude enough to masquerade as a solitary one. My name is on the cover. All mistakes in this volume are my own. But the best parts of my thinking are owed to the brilliant people who I can call friends: Jade Davis, Patricia A. Matthew, Melissa Creary, Roxane Gay, and Dorothy Brown push me to my highest self. They also make sure I leave enough of myself *for* myself. Lauren Garcia has provided me unparalleled research and support for this project. Hire her. My colleagues at Virginia Commonwealth University, where I teach and research as an assistant professor of sociology, provide me an intellectual space devoid of the petty politics that mar so many of our academic enclaves. Because they treat intellectual work as human labor, deserving of humane investment, I am able to do what I do.

And I do what I do because it is what I was put here to do. I am only sure about that and three other things in my entire life. Another of those things is that this work benefited greatly from the amazing scholarship of people like Beverly Guy-Sheftall, Patricia Hill Collins, Kimberlé Crenshaw, Joan Morgan, Brittney Cooper, Keeanga-Yamahtta Taylor, Desiree Melton, Adrian Piper, Christina Greer, and many, many others. That you hear more from these women's male counterparts in popular media than you do from them is a large part of why I do what I do. It has become in vogue to say "trust black women." One of the other things I know is that the time for choosing to do so has long passed. There is not a single global, national, or local condition to which black women's intellectual, spiritual, and emotional intelligences cannot be trusted to bring greater clarity. The 2016 election of Donald Trump joins the rise of nationalist, xenophobic, racist, sexist, and classist demagogues ascending to and consolidating power across the world. If not now, when?

NOTES

Thick

1. Roger Gomm and Martyn Hammersley, "Thick Ethnographic Description and Thin Models of Complexity," paper presented at the Annual Conference of the British Educational Research Association, University of Leeds, England, September 13–15, 2001, http://www.leeds.ac.uk/educol/documents/00001820.htm.

2. Tressie McMillan Cottom, "The Inferiority of Blackness as a Subject," *Tressiemc*, May 2, 2012, http://tressiemc.com/uncategorized/the-inferiority-of-blackness-as-a-subject.

3. Brittney C. Cooper, *Beyond Respectability: The Intellectual Thought of Race Women* (Chicago: University of Illinois Press, 2017); Brittney C. Cooper, *Eloquent Rage: A Black Feminist Discovers Her Superpower* (New York: St. Martin's Press, 2018); and Rebecca Traister, *Good and Mad: How Women's Anger Is Reshaping America* (New York: Simon and Schuster, 2018).

4. The Department of Labor puts it mildly when it says that "[h]istorically, Black women have had high labor force participation rates compared to other women" (2016). Despite entering the paid labor market at young ages and working for longer over our life course, black women have "less favorable outcomes than their White, non-Hispanic counterparts": lower wages, more frequent bouts of unemployment, a smaller share of the "good jobs" in the professional services sector,

and especially dismal representation in predicted high-wage jobs of the future like technology jobs. For more, see Women's Bureau at the United States Department of Labor, "Black Women in the Labor Force," February 2016.

5. Using data from the National Asset Scorecard for Communities of Color, a 2016 report by Darrick Hamilton, William Darity Jr., Anne E. Price, Vishnu Sridharan, and Rebecca Tippett finds that most black families have no more than $25 in liquid wealth, meaning money that they could easily access as opposed to wealth tied up in a home or investments. See Darrick Hamilton et al., "Umbrellas Don't Make It Rain: Why Studying and Working Hard Isn't Enough for Black Americans" (New York: The New School, 2015). Despite our pitiable wealth position, the W.K. Kellogg Foundation finds that African Americans give a larger share of their income to charities than any other group. With negligible wealth and lower rates of participation in high-income jobs, black families give. And when they give, black women are instrumental in encouraging how often, how much, and to whom they give. That is all the more impressive when one considers that this kind of charity rarely captures the in-kind services black women provide to churches, schools, and communities. For example, black women financially support family members who are incarcerated. See Natalie J. Sokoloff, "The Impact of the Prison Industrial Complex on African American Women," *Souls* 5, no. 4 (2003): 31–46; and Sandhya Dirks, "How Mass Incarceration Shapes the Lives of Black Women," KQED, July 6, 2016, https://www.kqed.org/news/11010927 /how-incarceration-shapes-the-lives-of-black-women.

6. In 2016, black women made up 61 percent of all students enrolled in historically black colleges and universities. They earned 50 percent of all degrees that HBCUs awarded that year, and black men earned 25 percent. (Author's calculations from table 313.30 of the Digest of Education Statistics, "Selected Statistics on Degree-Granting Historically Black Colleges and Universities, by Control and Level of Institution: Selected Years, 1990 through 2016.")

7. Whether single parents, coparents, or married, research has shown that black women disproportionately contribute to the economic and social well-being of their family units. The Center for American Progress's 2016 report on breadwinning women says that "black mothers are by far the most likely [group] to be the primary economic support for their families, both because they are more likely to be single mothers and because they are more likely—when part of a married couple—to earn as much as or more than their husbands." Sarah Jane Glynn, "Breadwinning Mothers Are Increasingly the U.S. Norm," Center for American Progress, December 19, 2016, http://www.americanprogress.org/issues/women/reports/2016/12/19/295203/breadwinning-mothers-are-increasingly-the-u-s-norm. See Rhonda Sharpe, Nina Banks, and Cecilia Conrad, *Black Women in the US Economy: The Hardest Working Woman* (New York: Routledge, forthcoming 2019).

8. For a host of reasons, both economic and cultural, black women's political participation is a critical part of modern electoral politics. In 2012, black women voted at a higher rate than any other group according to the Center for American Progress. Maya Harris, "Women of Color: A Growing Force in the American Electorate," Center for American Progress, October 30, 2014, http://www.americanprogress.org/issues/race/reports/2014/10/30/99962/women-of-color.

Indeed, had white women's participation been equivalent, we may have seen a different presidential result in 2016. Beyond electoral politics, black women's civic participation spans the entire U.S. history. For a starting point on that literature, see Melissa V. Harris-Perry, *Sister Citizen: Shame, Stereotypes, and Black Women in America* (New Haven, CT, and London: Yale University Press, 2011).

9. In social movements, new research makes a clear case that black women have also been central to building and sustaining black social movements. To read more, see Ashley D. Farmer, *Remaking Black Power: How Black Women Transformed an Era* (Chapel Hill: University of North Carolina Press, 2017); and Danielle L. McGuire, *At the Dark End of the*

NOTES

Street: Black Women, Rape, and Resistance—a New History of the Civil Rights Movement from Rosa Parks to the Rise of Black Power (New York: Knopf, 2010). The Black Lives Matter movement has made notable inroads in renegotiating the invisible labor of black women in movement work. To learn more about that struggle, see activist Patrisse Khan-Cullors's memoir with Asha Bandele, *When They Call You a Terrorist: A Black Lives Matter Memoir* (New York: St. Martin's Press, 2018).

10. Isabel Wilkerson, *The Warmth of Other Suns: The Epic Story of America's Great Migration* (New York: Vintage, 2011).

11. Predatory tax assessment schemes have been used to extract black wealth for generations. It continues apace today. Although much is made about how the foreclosure crisis of the 2010s decimated black household wealth and security, racist schemes at local municipal levels have been doing much the same for generations. For examples of this in practice see Kriston Capps, "How the Black Tax Destroyed African American Home-ownership in Chicago," *CityLab*, June 11, 2015; and Leah Douglas, "African Americans Have Lost Untold Acres of Land over the Last Century," *The Nation*, June 26, 2017. The shadow of these stories trailed every black family I knew, including my own, like a bogeyman. As a result, every year our family gathered in fear, intent on raising enough money to pay taxes for a plot of land we owned in an undeveloped part of North Carolina. Even paying the taxes never got rid of the fear entirely. That, of course, is the point of systemic legal racist terrorism: to keep people like us living in fear.

12. For more on the racial hierarchy of the rural eastern North Carolina region where my family is from, see Malinda Maynor Lowery, *Lumbee Indians in the Jim Crow South: Race, Identity, and the Making of a Nation* (Chapel Hill: University of North Carolina Press, 2010).

13. Cooper hails the discursive politics of respectability in black women's lived experiences of political economy: Brittney C. Cooper, *Beyond Respectability: The Intellectual Thought of Race Women* (Champagne,

IL: University of Illinois Press, 2017). Evelyn Brooks Higginbotham, "Beyond The Sound of Silence: Afro-American Women in History," *Gender & History* 1, no. 1 (1989): 50–67.

14. Jia Tolentino, "The Personal-Essay Boom Is Over," *New Yorker,* September 18, 2017.

15. Michelle Barrow, "It Happened to Me: My Gynecologist Found a Ball of Cat Hair in My Vagina," *xoJane,* March 27, 2017, https://www.xojane.com/it-happened-to-me/my-gynecologist-found-a-ball-of-cat-hair-in-my-vagina.

16. For an excellent, far-reaching primer of how money is a social relationship that shapes our understanding of what is good or moral, start with sociologist Viviana Zelizer's *Economic Lives: How Culture Shapes the Economy* (Princeton, NJ: Princeton University Press, 2010).

17. Stacia L. Brown, "The Personal Essay Economy Offers Fewer Rewards for Black Women," *The New Republic,* September 18, 2015.

In the Name of Beauty

1. bell hooks, *Art on My Mind: Visual Politics* (New York: The New Press, 1995). hooks is interested in the aesthetics of art and culture in this lovely meditation on beauty. I extrapolate from her work here to the idea of embodied and structural beauty. For more on that, see Heather Widdows, *Perfect Me: Beauty as an Ethical Ideal* (Princeton, NJ: Princeton University Press, 2018).

2. Pierre Bourdieu, *The Logic of Practice* (Stanford, CA: Stanford University Press, 1990).

3. Tressie McMillan Cottom, "When Your (Brown) Body Is a (White) Wonderland," *Tressiemc,* August 27, 2013, http://tressiemc.com/uncategorized/when-your-brown-body-is-a-white-wonderland.

4. McMillan Cottom, "When Your (Brown) Body Is a (White) Wonderland." No less than the great modern essayist Ta-Nehisi Coates has

called his HBCU, Howard University, a "mecca." His is an allusion to the history of black colleges as safe spaces for African Americans in a hostile white society. It is also symbolic of the way many African Americans understand the history of HBCUs: beacons on a hill that promise meritocracy for black people shut out, by definition, from the very idea of being meritorious in white institutions. I responded to Coates's ode to his mecca with my own meditation on historically black college life as a heterosexual, femme black woman. HBCUs are safe spaces for developing one's racial self, for actualizing an identity not predicated on racial hierarchy, and for building capacity for black knowledge production. But I am not only black. I am a black woman of working-class origins and enslaved genealogy. Meccas are complicated for people like me. At my HBCU I navigated black enlightenment and sexual violence; classism and community organizing; colorism and favorable mate markets. There remain other versions of mecca—being queer, being undocumented, being trans, being conservative, being a socialist, being a number of other things that we are in various configurations while also being black. I always speak of black institutions like I speak of black people: the highest faith in our humanity is not to imagine us as idyllic gods but beautifully flawed humans. Tressie McMillan Cottom, "'Between the World and Me' Book Club: The Stories Untold," *The Atlantic*, August 3, 2015. Ta-Nehisi Coates, "Letter to My Son," *The Atlantic*, July 4, 2015.

5. Limor Shifman, *Memes in Digital Culture* (Cambridge, MA: MIT Press, 2014).

6. Kate M. Miltner, "'There's No Place for Lulz on LOLCats'": The Role of Genre, Gender, and Group Identity in the Interpretation and Enjoyment of an Internet Meme," *First Monday* 19, no. 8 (2014).

7. Naomi Wolf, *The Beauty Myth: How Images of Beauty Are Used Against Women* (New York: Random House, 2013).

NOTES

8. Barbara Trepagnier, "The Politics of White and Black Bodies," *Feminism & Psychology* 4, no. 1 (1994): 199–205. Trepagnier calls it "the unspoken whiteness of the beauty myth." Margaret Hunter brings some empirical heft to how white beauty ideals operate through colorism, or the hierarchical status of skin color, from light to dark. Hunter argues that nonwhite women's socioeconomic well-being is stratified in part through their ability to legitimately claim proximity to white beauty standards. Margaret L. Hunter, "Colorstruck: Skin Color Stratification in the Lives of African American Women," *Sociological Inquiry* 68, no. 4 (1998): 517–35; and Margaret L. Hunter, "'If You're Light You're Alright': Light Skin Color as Social Capital for Women of Color," *Gender & Society* 16, no. 2 (2002): 175–93.

Meeta Jha gives a global perspective on this, demonstrating how ideas of whiteness and beauty stratify the life chances of women across the globe. Meeta Jha, *The Global Beauty Industry: Colorism, Racism, and the National Body* (New York: Routledge, 2015). The gist is this: the beauty myth is hell on white women's sovereignty and it makes white women's lives empirically better than those of nonwhite women in the United States and across the globe. The latter is true because the former is made true through the U.S. military and economic and cultural domination.

9. Sidestepping many of Wolf's blind spots are a book by Jessica Valenti, *The Purity Myth: How America's Obsession with Virginity Is Hurting Young Women* (Berkeley, CA: Seal Press, 2009); and this essay, which I love: Lili Loofbourow, "The Female Price of Male Pleasure," *The Week*, January 25, 2018, http://theweek.com/articles/749978/female-price-male -pleasure.

10. Patricia Hill Collins, *Black Sexual Politics: African Americans, Gender, and the New Racism* (New York: Routledge, 2004).

11. You could do worse than to spend some time reading more recent scholarship from black feminist thought that tackles post-deindustrialization culture. To start:

Tricia Rose, *Black Noise: Rap Music and Black Culture in Contemporary America*, vol. 6 (Middletown, CT: Wesleyan University Press, 1994).

Joan Morgan, *When Chickenheads Come Home to Roost: A Hip-Hop Feminist Breaks It Down* (New York: Simon and Schuster, 2017).

Gwendolyn D. Pough, *Check It While I Wreck It: Black Womanhood, Hip-Hop Culture, and the Public Sphere* (Lebanon, NH: Northeastern University Press, 2015).

Imani Perry, *Prophets of the Hood: Politics and Poetics in Hip Hop* (Durham, NC: Duke University Press, 2004).

Brittney Cooper, *Eloquent Rage: A Black Feminist Discovers Her Superpower* (New York: St. Martin's Press, 2018).

T. Denean Sharpley-Whiting, *Pimps Up, Ho's Down: Hip Hop's Hold on Young Black Women* (New York: New York University Press, 2008).

12. "SNL Under Fire After Slavery Skit," MSNBC, http://www.msnbc.com/the-last-word/watch/snl-under-fire-after-slavery-skit-247630403748. Tressie McMillan Cottom, "Here, a Hypocrite Lives: I Probably Get It Wrong on Leslie Jones but I Tried," *Tressiemc*, May 6, 2014, https://tressiemc.com/uncategorized/here-a-hypocrite-lives-i-probably-get-it-wrong-on-leslie-jones-but-i-tried.

13. An important and notable exception is Joan Morgan's recent turn in theorizing a black feminist politics of pleasure. See more at Joan Morgan, "Why We Get Off: Moving Towards a Black Feminist Politics of Pleasure," *The Black Scholar* 45, no. 4 (2015): 36–46.

NOTES

14. Beauty has an attendant religious doctrine, perfected through white western women who are its ideal consumers and site of what we sociologists call prosumption, the new-economy exchange where market actors simultaneously produce and consume monetized cultural forms. We are consumers when we buy a smartphone. We become prosumers when the data we transact through our smartphones produces a new product or idea or consumer good. We co-create goods with those who own its value at our expense. That is prosumption. The elegance of our appified, digitally mediated, late-stage capitalism is that producing beauty feels empowering and obscures how we are also consuming beauty produced by others. When I said that I was unattractive, I violated a prime directive of gender that, if I were allowed to do without penalty, undermines the ideology of beauty. Challengers pushed me on the value of my "inner beauty," which is the kind that can be achieved through the conspicuous consumption of the right books, right media, and right makeup.

15. It fell outside the scope of my biography-structure argument in this book, but it is important to note that the idea of beauty, especially presentation as femme and nonwhite, has a particular set of politics for trans women of color and black trans women. For more on that, see Michael Lovelock: "Problematically, I argue, this process has worked to demarcate ideals of 'acceptable' transgender subjectivity: self-sufficient, normatively feminine, and eager to embrace the possibilities for happiness and social integration provided by the commercial domain." "Call Me Caitlyn: Making and Making over the 'Authentic' Transgender Body in Anglo-American Popular Culture," *Journal of Gender Studies* 26, no. 6 (2017): 675–87.

And, in her essay on "pretty" as a privilege, Janet Mock issues several provocations that I hope are taken further by other writers. Namely, what does femme beauty politics mean when colorism and ethnocentric beauty hierarchies delimit one's presentation of a socially acceptable "real" woman, to borrow from Mock's social media hashtag? For more on that provocation, read Sarah Beauchamp, "Janet Mock Breaks Down the Uncomfortable Truth of Pretty Girl Privilege," *Nylon*, June 28, 2017, https://nylon.com/articles/janet-mock-pretty-privilege.

16. In general, black people are more likely to interact with the criminal justice system, and to receive harsher sentences when they do so. See United States Sentencing Commission, "Demographic Differences in Federal Sentencing Practices: An Update of the Booker Report's Multivariate Regression Analysis" (2010). Black students are more likely to be disciplined in schools and more punitively than nonblack students. Nathan Barrett, Andrew McEachin, Jonathan Mills, and Jon Valant, "Discipline Disparities and Discrimination in Schools," Brookings, January 9, 2018; and Tom Loveless, "Racial Disparities in School Suspensions," Brookings, April 6, 2018.

Black women are the least likely group to marry someone of another race, one oft-cited sign of racial "acceptance." See Kristen Bialik, "Key Facts About Race and Marriage, 50 Years After Loving v. Virginia," Pew Research Center, June 12, 2017, http://www.pewresearch.org/fact-tank /2017/06/12/key-facts-about-race-and-marriage-50-years-after-loving -v-virginia. Richard V. Reeves and Katherine Guyot, "Black Women Are Earning More College Degrees, but That Alone Won't Close Race Gaps," Brookings, December 8, 2017, http://www.brookings.edu/blog/social -mobility-memos/2017/12/04/black-women-are-earning-more-college -degrees-but-that-alone-wont-close-race-gaps.

Yet even these statistical trends are not equally true for all black men and women. Research shows that skin color also mediates the severity of social stigma and exclusion. Darker-complexioned black people are more likely to be members of lower social status and experience higher rates of housing segregation, and are less likely to be employed in high-status work than their lighter black counterparts. And recent research shows that darker-skinned black women are less likely to marry and when they do so are less likely to marry an economic peer than are lighter-skinned

NOTES

black women. Even in criminal justice, the multiple marginality of skin tone, race, gender, and social class shows up: darker-skinned black women convicted of criminal offenses receive harsher sentences than do lighter black women. Skin color matters. See Jill Viglione, Lance Hannon, and Robert DeFina, "The Impact of Light Skin on Prison Time for Black Female Offenders," *Social Science Journal* 48, no. 1 (2011): 250–58; Ellis P. Monk Jr, "Skin Tone Stratification Among Black Americans, 2001–2003," *Social Forces* 92, no. 4 (2014): 1313–37; and Zhenchao Qian, "Breaking the Last Taboo: Interracial Marriage in America," *Contexts* 4, no. 4 (2005): 33–37.

Dying to Be Competent

1. Michel Foucault, *Society Must Be Defended: Lectures at the Collège de France, 1975–76,* trans. David Macey (New York: Picador, 2003).

2. Speaking with a business writer, LinkedIn founder Reid Hoffman intimated that many people use the platform wrong when they automatically accept any request. See more at http://www.businessinsider.com/reid -hoffman-how-to-use-linkedin-2017-4.

3. World Health Organization, "World Health Statistics 2014: A Wealth of Information on Global Public Health" (2014).

4. "Pregnancy Related Mortality," Centers for Disease Control and Prevention, May 9, 2018, http://www.cdc.gov/reproductivehealth /maternalinfanthealth/pregnancy-relatedmortality.htm.

5. "Infant Mortality," Centers for Disease Control and Prevention, August 3, 2018, www.cdc.gov/reproductivehealth/maternalinfanthealth /infantmortality.htm.

6. More than just stereotypes, controlling images are racialized, gendered, and classed ideologies produced by and through social institutions

such as the media but also through political bodies, educational institutions, and courts.

7. Because I refuse to believe in the concept as anything other than a political designation, I use it here the way it is used loosely in popular culture—amorphous, apolitical, and ambivalent about the project of ending anti-blackness. Tamara K. Nopper has great work on how the idea of "people of color" as a category marshals important resources to the detriment of black small business owners: "Minority, Black, and Non-Black People of Color: 'New' Color-Blind Racism and the US Small Business Administration's Approach to Minority Business Lending in the Post-Civil Rights Era," *Critical Sociology* 37, no. 5 (2011): 651–71. And sociologist Jared Sexton calls the erasure of anti-blackness that can be embedded in the elisions of "people of color" endemic to the political construct of the term: "People-of-Color-Blindness Notes on the Afterlife of Slavery," *Social Text* 28, no. 2 (2010): 31–56.

8. Patricia Hill Collins, "Black Feminist Thought in the Matrix of Domination," *Social Theory: The Multicultural and Classic Readings* (1993): 615–25.

Know Your Whites

1. Cheryl I. Harris, "Whiteness as Property," *Harvard Law Review* (1993): 1707–91.

2. Carol Anderson, *White Rage: The Unspoken Truth of Our Racial Divide* (New York: Bloomsbury, 2016).

3. This should tell you everything you need to know about the neighborhood. Thinking sociologically, if you know an urban, suburban, or exurban rate of housing price change, foreclosure rates post–Great Recession, and type of neighborhood infrastructure, you should be able to intuit the community's racial and economic makeup. A stable community like this one correlates with wealth, which correlates with race in the United

NOTES

States. That is how we experience structural wealth inequality in our everyday lives.

4. R. L'Heureux Lewis-McCoy, *Inequality in the Promised Land: Race, Resources, and Suburban Schooling* (Stanford, CA: Stanford University Press, 2014). Amanda E. Lewis and John B. Diamond, *Despite the Best Intentions: How Racial Inequality Thrives in Good Schools* (Oxford and New York: Oxford University Press, 2015).

5. Nonwhite voters went heavily for Barack Obama in both 2008 and 2012, but there were some differences within those groups. Black voters overwhelmingly voted for Obama across class, immigrant status, education, and income level. There were minor variations among Asian Americans of different national origins. For example, South Asian American voters were more solidly Obama voters than other ethnic groups. See the Asian American Legal Defense and Education Fund report, "The Asian American Vote 2012." There are similar differences among Hispanics by national origin and generational status. See Mark Hugo Lopez and Paul Taylor, "Dissecting the 2008 Electorate: Most Diverse in U.S. History," Pew Research Center's Hispanic Trends Project, April 30, 2009, http://www.pewhispanic.org/2009/04/30/dissecting-the-2008-electorate-most-diverse-in-us-history.

6. Ta-Nehisi Coates, *We Were Eight Years in Power: An American Tragedy* (New York: One World/Ballantine, 2017).

7. "Obama's Legacy: Diss-ent or Diss-respect?" *Codeswitch* podcast, NPR, http://www.npr.org/sections/codeswitch/2017/02/23/51681/8239/obamas-legacy-diss-ent-or-diss-respect.

8. Ta-Nehisi Coates, "My President Was Black," *The Atlantic*, January, 2017.

9. I have discussed how euphemisms for racism, like *racial*, discursively obscure actors that enact racism. For more, see http://progressivenetwork.wordpress.com/tag/tressie-mcmillan-cottom.

NOTES

10. Robin DiAngelo's "White Fragility" framing looms large in our current discourse. It is a useful analytical framework to help us think through how white racial identity emerges as something that must always be protected, even, or especially, at the expense of nonwhites. Still, naming white innocence "fragile" belies its fundamental nature, which is domination. The performance of fragility can only be done to great effect because whiteness necessarily dominates and oppresses. Whiteness isn't then fragile, but blunt; not vulnerable, but resilient.

11. I remember the Katt Williams version of this joke, but Chris Rock did a version of it four years before. You could do worse than to watch both: Katt Williams, "It's Pimpin' Pimpin'," 2008, http://www.dailymotion.com /video/x5wd5w0, at 32:40. Chris Rock, "Never Scared," 2004, http:// scrapsfromtheloft.com/2018/01/19/chris-rock-never-scared-2004-full -transcript, at 23:16.

Black Is Over (Or, Special Black)

1. If U.S.-ians had ever reckoned with enslavement and apartheid we might have become sophisticated enough by now to have a public discourse that could talk about both race and ethnicity. Alas, here we are. For a working schema, race is socially constructed *and* also biologically marked. Race refers to those biological characteristics—hair, skin tone, features—that have been socially constructed as distinct and cohesive. Ethnicity refers to the shared cultural symbols, rituals, and beliefs that a group primarily self-selects into. One often inherits their culture from their families much like one inherits their biological race markers. But, because we are social beings all implicated in how race is made, one can generally exercise more agency in selecting their cultural identity than they can their racial identity. Black people have both a racial and an ethnic identity. It is only because blackness is so totalizing as a racial ideology (to legitimize the existence of whiteness) that we rarely think of black people as an ethnic

group. For more, see this accessible video by sociologist Tanya Golash-Boza, "What Is Race? What Is Ethnicity? What Is the Difference?," http://vimeo.com/286520524.

2. Sara Ahmed, *On Being Included: Racism and Diversity in Institutional Life* (Durham, NC: Duke University Press, 2012).

3. In one of the more perversely delightful studies of recent memory, this article about diversity and college websites finds that "78% of institutions used photos that overrepresented the percentage of minorities at the institution." Jeffery L. Wilson, and Katrina A. Meyer, "Higher Education Websites: The 'Virtual Face' of Diversity," *Journal of Diversity in Higher Education* 2, no. 2 (2009): 91.

4. Political scientist Candis Watts Smith says in her larger study of black ethnic immigrants that approximately 40 percent of those identified as black enrolled in Ivy League colleges are black immigrants. Candis Watts Smith, *Black Mosaic: The Politics of Black Pan-ethnic Diversity* (New York: New York University Press, 2014).

The Price of Fabulousness

1. Michael Scaturro, "He Literally Wrote the Book on Fabulousness," *New York Times*, June 8, 2018.

2. Rita Kiki Edozie and Curtis Stokes, eds., *Malcolm X's Michigan Worldview: An Exemplar for Contemporary Black Studies* (East Lansing: Michigan State University Press, 2015).

3. White people calling the police on black people in 2018: an abridged timeline:

April 12, barista calls police on black men at Starbucks:
http://www.eater.com/2018/4/27/17263584/starbucks-arrests
-third-place

April 21, white man calls police on group of black women golfers:
https://www.cbsnews.com/news/grandview-golf-club-man-who
-called-police-on-black-women-golfers-denies-racism

April 30, white woman calls police on three black people exiting
their Airbnb rental:
https://www.facebook.com/directedbykells/posts
/10160498802675121

May 8, white woman calls police on black Yale student for sleep-
ing in common area:
https://www.nytimes.com/2018/05/09/nyregion/yale-black
-student-nap.html

June 4, black woman arrested after white woman falsely accuses
her of shoplifting:
https://wreg.com/2018/06/07/woman-says-she-was-racially
-profiled-at-victorias-secret-in-collierville

June 23, white woman calls police on black twelve-year-old mow-
ing grass:
https://www.washingtonpost.com/news/post-nation/wp/2018
/06/30/a-white-woman-called-police-on-a-black-12-year-old-for
-mowing-grass

June 23, white woman calls police on black teens at pool:
https://www.facebook.com/rhema.inhislyfe/posts
/10100550190183435

June 23, white woman calls police on eight-year-old black girl
selling water:
https://twitter.com/_ethiopiangold/status
/1010577140595560448

July 1, white woman calls police on black woman for smoking
cigarette:
https://www.theroot.com/newportnancy-wants-black-neighbor
-evicted-for-smoking-1827320227

July 2, white woman calls police on family of seven eating dinner: https://www.yahoo.com/lifestyle/eating-black-subway-calls -police-family-using-restroom-many-times-180331037.html

July 4, white man calls police on black mother and baby at pool: https://nypost.com/2018/07/06/white-man-loses-job-after-calling -police-on-black-family-at-pool

July 13, white man calls police on black woman trying to use coupon at CVS: https://www.buzzfeednews.com/article/remysmidt/white -cvs-employee-cvs-calls-cops-black-woman-using-coupon# .cikxA0d19

July 17, white man calls police on black man for fouling him during a basketball game: https://nypost.com/2018/07/17/man-calls-cops-after-hard-foul-in -pickup-basketball-game

July 25, white woman calls police on black woman waiting for an Uber in the rain: https://www.theroot.com/brooklyn-becky-cops-called-on -suspicious-looking-black-1828057076

4. Jim Walter Homes sold manufactured home "kits." For a little money down one could also lease land for the home through the company. The company went out of business in 2009, but not before half of my extended relations begged, borrowed, and stole for their own Jim Walter–branded piece of the American Dream. Read more about the history of this manufactured home builder here: http://www.searshomes.org/index.php/tag /jim-walter-homes.

Black Girlhood, Interrupted

1. Ruth Nicole Brown, *Black Girlhood Celebration: Toward a Hip-Hop Feminist Pedagogy* (New York: Peter Lang, 2009).

NOTES

2. Anne Moody, *Coming of Age in Mississippi* (New York: Dell, 2004).

3. Monique Morris, *Pushout: The Criminalization of Black Girls in Schools* (New York: The New Press, 2016).

4. Rebecca Epstein, Jamilia Blake, and Thalia Gonzalez, "Girlhood Interrupted: The Erasure of Black Girls' Childhood," June 27, 2017.

5. Abbie Bennett, "'NC Is the Only State Where No Doesn't Mean No': Court Case Ruled Women Can't Back Out of Sex," *News & Observer*, June 22, 2017, http://www.newsobserver.com/news/politics-government/state-politics/article157694194.html.

6. Women generally are not considered reliable subjects in the criminal justice system. Feminist legal scholars have shown this repeatedly and often using examples of how women are expected to perform domesticity in cases of domestic violence. For black women that performance is complicated by the science and legal practices used to argue domestic cases. These cases often rely on medical testimony or records of abuse to corroborate women's testimony. Standard medical practice relies on observable evidence of abuse to create that bureaucratic evidence trail. This includes using tools to capture images of bruises and relying on doctors' and nurses' visual inspection for bruises. Both of these methods systematically underidentify domestic violence in black women because bruising of dark skin is harder to identify and rarely adjusted for in medical imaging equipment. As a consequence, black women who are already constructed as unreliable legal subjects are also constructed as un-abusable medical subjects. This leaves black women more vulnerable to domestic abuse and less likely to receive legal or medical assistance for that abuse. To learn more, see Adele M. Morrison, "Changing the Domestic Violence (Dis)course: Moving from White Victim to Multi-cultural Survivor," *UC Davis Law Review* 39 (March 2006): 1061, on how the medical system and legal system construct female subjects in domestic violence cases. And see how proposed

innovations in the equipment used to scan for bruising could provide better screening for black women, especially darker-skinned black women: "Rochester Team Casts Light on a Hidden Problem in Domestic Violence Cases," *University of Rochester Newscenter,* July 26, 2018, http://www.rochester.edu/newscenter/rochester-team-casts-light-hidden-problem-domestic-violence-291592.

7. Charlamagne Tha God, *Black Privilege: Opportunity Comes to Those Who Create It* (New York: Simon and Schuster, 2018), 107.

Girl 6

1. Coretta Pittman, "Black Women Writers and the Trouble with Ethos: Harriet Jacobs, Billie Holiday, and Sister Souljah," *Rhetoric Society Quarterly* 37, no. 1 (2006): 43–70.

2. David Brooks, "How We Are Ruining America," *New York Times,* July 11, 2017.

3. There is not a nice way around this, so I will just say it. There is a prestige hierarchy in media. Whether we like it or not, a top tier of publications exist and they do influence public opinion and media punditry. Classic studies in sociology of what we call "interlocking directorates," or the powerful economic and cultural institutions that shape hegemonic elite discourse, exist. New media has fragmented that reality somewhat but not entirely.

4. Tressie McMillan Cottom, *Lower Ed: The Troubling Rise of For-Profit Colleges in the New Economy* (New York: The New Press, 2017).

5. In May 2018, a federal judge decided it was unconstitutional for Trump to block people on Twitter while he is president: http://www.cnbc.com/2018/05/23/trump-cant-block-twitter-followers-federal-judge-says.html.

6. Bill Heil and Mikolaj Piskorski, "New Twitter Research: Men Follow Men and Nobody Tweets," *Harvard Business Review* 1 (2009), http://hbr.org/2009/06/new-twitter-research-men-follo.

7. Jake Johnson, "Bringing on Badly Needed 'Prophetic Voice,' New York Times Hires Michelle Alexander as Full-Time Columnist," *Common Dreams*, June 21, 2018, http://www.commondreams.org/news/2018/06/21/bringing-badly-needed-prophetic-voice-new-york-times-hires-michelle-alexander-full.

8. Michelle Alexander, *The New Jim Crow: Mass Incarceration in the Age of Colorblindness* (New York: The New Press, 2009).